What the Best Managers
Know and Do

Also by Terry Joseph Busch

Effective Corporate Decision Making:
Six Steps to Success

Habits That Define Poor Managers:
A Rogues Gallery

Effective Organizational Leadership:
The Essential Ingredients

An Executive Trail Guide:
Thinking and Behaving For Success

Terry Joseph Busch

What the Best Managers Know and Do

iv

Library of Congress Control Number: 2018900446

Dedication

To encouraging more enlightened managers and leaders.

To my darling wife Paulette, our son Joseph, and our daughter Andrea. The unwavering love and support each of you has given me over the years enabled the journey that led to this book.

Acknowledgment

As any honest author will tell you, there comes a point where we can no longer evaluate our own prose, clarity of message, and consistent adherence to the dictates of accepted punctuation and grammar rules. I asked my dear friend Mary Evjen to give this book the gift of her keen mind, professional writing experience, and willingness to offer critical advice when necessary. The pages to follow have benefited enormously from her efforts. I am and will remain ever grateful for her contributions.

Contents

It's one of the characteristics of a leader that he not doubt for one moment the capacity of the people he's leading to realize whatever he's dreaming. Imagine if Martin Luther King had said, I have a dream. Of course, I'm not sure they'll be up to it.

Benjamin Zander

Forward

This book represents a summary and synthesis of what I have experienced, observed and learned during my years as a manager, executive, and consultant. I have likewise learned a great deal from the hundreds of participants who have shared their wisdom in my Management Workshops. I share some of that wisdom here as well.

I have divided the book's discussions into sections that parallel the structure of my management workshop, which shares the same title. Each section represents a critical requirement for effective management.

I begin with a discussion of my discovering the reality of what it means to be a manager and the work ethic that characterizes all those who eventually warrant the sobriquet *good manager.* I then turn my attention to the critical importance of self-management and the never-ending challenge of being responsible for the performance of human beings.

In the middle sections, I explore the true significance of agreeing to shoulder and exercise the responsibility of a manager and share some of the practices the best managers use to unlock the talent and potential of those entrusted to their management skills.

In the concluding sections, I address the many obstacles we face in making ourselves understood by those we oversee, the fundamental importance of the learning and practice required to become a top notch management professional, and provide a series of typical management scenarios for readers to analyze and decide how they would confront the various challenges and conundrums each of them presents

I suggest you may find this book best read a section at a time. That way, you can take a moment to reflect on a discrete, core element of the management profession and evaluate your own thoughts and approach. If I have done my job well, you may wish to keep this book handy as a quick reference when you confront your inevitable variations of the topics contained in its sections.

I have tried my best not to be preachy or overly prescriptive. I do not believe in telling adults what to do. They usually resist that sort of thing, often angrily. Most of us are at our best when we work things out for ourselves and find those strategies that suit us best. My goal in this book is to stimulate thinking that accelerates and enriches your own thought processes.

Feel free to disagree with anything I say or suggest in this book. I encourage other points of view. I barely have figured out some of the right questions to ask in many management situations, much less discovered the best answers.

When you disagree, have a firm point of view supported by your own experiences. Opinions are cheap, we all have them. Our facts are generally hard won through trail and error.

There are no right answers to the challenges of being a manager. Most of what we do rests on acts of faith that our course of action will work. It is what happens once we have done something – the facts our experiences produce – that tell us whether it was a good idea or not.

As author and novelist Bernard Malamud and the Glenn Close character in the movie *The Natural* remind us: *We have two lives... the life we learn with and the life we live after that.* Of all the insights I have gained about managing, none is more important than understanding the best managers never stop learning and applying the lessons they have learned to the benefit of those they serve.

What the Best Managers Know and Do

Primum Non Nocere

First, do no harm

1.

Discovering Reality

We live in a fantasy world, a world of Illusion.
The great task in life is to find reality.

Irish author Iris Murdoch

This job is way harder than I thought it would be.

Millions of new managers

What is it that separates the best managers from the rest? Why do some managers seem to grasp their job and do the correct thing, while others make more mistakes?

I have been pondering these questions for many years. I started thinking about them from the start of my management career and discovered I needed to confront the fundamental mis-perception I brought to my first management assignment.

Like so many other new managers, I simply assumed the job represented a small next step in my professional career. I had worked for many managers and to my way of thinking, their job did not seem that hard. Hand out assignments, provide guidance and instructions, counsel and coach people, review the work of others, grant some pay raises, and ensure your employees are working. How difficult could that be?

My mis-perception was a failure to grasp that I had entered a completely new profession; a profession I had neither been educated nor trained for and a profession whose requirements for success I did not understand.

About halfway through my first year, I figuratively hit the wall. While panic may be too strong a word, I certainly felt anxious and overwhelmed.

I began to realize that I could not easily explain why I was doing anything I was doing. Put another way, I didn't know *what the hell I was doing.* I was simply reacting to things rather than thinking through things. I was micromanaging to avoid making mistakes, blindly taking on everything coming my way rather than establishing priorities, and I was beginning the deadly cycle of second-guessing almost everything I did.

I knew things had to change and realized I had two choices. I could quit and return to my previous profession in which I had achieved some success. Or, I could accept the fact that I was a management neophyte with a great deal to learn and initiate the process my education would require. I chose the latter.

I will avoid an extended discussion of the many colleagues and mentors who took pity on me and helped shepherd my education. There were many of them, as there are in the stories of most successful professionals. Their unconditional support was essential to my development. The most important thing they taught me was the necessity of becoming a dedicated learner, a subject I will return to later in this book.

It was at this critical early stage in my management career I began to seek the recipe for the secret sauce; the secrets explaining why the best managers around me always seemed to know what to do, while many others often did not.

While management training, education, reading in the field, and collaboration with one's colleagues all seemed important contributors to a manager's development, I began to realize there was still something more the best managers seemed to know and consequently use as a guide.

This book is about what I gradually discovered. The real secret involves the intuitive grasp the best managers have for the essential requirements for being a good and effective manager.

By intuitive grasp, I do not mean they have read about management, taken good notes in management classes and committed them to memory. Nor do I mean they can say the right things when talking about management with others. Many managers can do that. Many managers have a solid intellectual grasp of management theories and concepts and an abstract understanding of what they are supposed to do, but little feel for how to turn their knowledge into the correct action.

The best managers grasp the job both intellectually and emotionally. Deep down they have a well-developed, experience-based, intuitive understanding of the basic core elements of their profession. They have an empathic feel for it in their bones as they say, in ways many of their colleagues do not.

Being a great manager does not mean you are smarter, taller, better looking, male or female. Moreover, the good ones I have known were not necessarily top-notch managers right from the start.

While some individuals may begin with some natural intellectual and personal assets that predispose them to succeed as managers, all the good ones understand they must learn and continually hone their craft over time.

What is it that sets the very best managers apart from the rest? Read on.

2.

The work Ethic

Amateurs hope, Professionals work.

American author Garson Kanin

Managing is an extremely hard and sometimes thankless job. It is inherently a humbling experience. It is a profession never fully mastered. Beyond just having the right grasp and feel for the management profession, the best managers know they will need to work hard.

In this regard, I find four different authors, instructive. Focusing on different topics and writing almost two decades apart, all agreed upon the extreme value of practice and hard work when it comes to professional success.

In 1990, Washington Post columnist George Will published *Men at Work.*[1] His subject was baseball, a sport Hall of Fame pitcher Warren Spahn describes as *a game of failure, even the best batters fail about 65% of the time.*[2] Will's description of the game and its players and managers illustrates how mastering their craft amounts to the constant repetition of the essential skills of their profession. Craftsmanship requires concentrated skill practice and hard work.

Psychologist Carol Dweck, in her book *Mind Set: The New Psychology of success,*[3] focuses her attention on a group of individuals who approach their intelligence and abilities as if they were muscles. The harder you work them the stronger they become. These individuals, she argues, tend to work harder, see mistakes as learning opportunities, and willingly and happily accept new challenges. They work

---

1   George F. Will, *Men At Work* (New York: Macmillan, 1960) .

2   Ibid., 1.

3   Carol Dweck, *Mind Set: The New Psychology of Success,* (New York: Random House, 2006).

diligently at getting better at what they have chosen to do in their lives, thereby significantly improving their chances of achieving success.

Malcolm Gladwell's book *Outliers* focuses on a series of truly exceptional contemporary performers, each of whom had considerable talent and sometimes-extraordinary opportunities aiding their path to success. However, in a chapter entitled *The 10,000-Hour Rule*, Gladwell presents a strong case that what often distinguishes one top performer from another is how hard they work. And what's more, he writes, "the people at the very top don't work just harder or even much harder than everyone else. They work much, much harder."[4] They have put in at least 10,000 hours worth of practicing their craft before being considered expert at what they do.

Finally, consider Geoffrey Colvin's *Talent is Overrated: What Really Separates World Class Performers from Everybody Else*.[5] Colvin does not dismiss the importance of talent or opportunity when it comes to success. He believes talent alone isn't enough. He argues persuasively for the importance of what he calls deliberate practice when it comes to distinguishing those best able to exploit an opportunity and their talent. By deliberate practice, Colvin refers to a process involving concentration on those things your profession demands you improve, practicing them

---

4   Malcolm Gladwell, *Outliers*, (New York: Little Brown and Company, 2008), 39.

5   Geoffrey Colvin, *Talent Is Overrated: What Really Separates World Class Performance from Everybody Else*, (New York: Portfolio, Random House Publishing, updated Edition, 2010).

specifically, evaluating the outcomes, and then making each of the necessary adjustments required.

The best managers in my experience all seemed to have an intuitive understanding of the wisdom these four authors capture. The best managers do more than just work hard, they hone in on the core skills of the management profession and practice to improve how they execute them. They honestly assess their performances, they identify their strengths and weaknesses, and work assiduously to improve. They seek out the feedback of others and strive to make adjustments when necessary.

We all can't be top performers in our field. However, work at any craft or profession 40 hours a week, 48 weeks of the year and that's 1,920 hours of work per annum. In five years you are almost at the 10,000-hour mark; 9,600 hours to be precise. That's a lot of practice, enough to make anyone much better at anything.

3.

Managing Yourself

Man who man would be,
must rule the empire of himself.

Percy Bysshe Shelley

Early in my management workshops, I ask participants who is the most important individual you must learn how to manage? They almost never get the answer wrong. *Myself,* they say. But I ask, do you understand how difficult a life-long struggle this task is for most of us? Some do but many I suspect do not. What seems so obvious appears to be beyond the capability of many Homo sapiens as judged by the frequent repetition of dysfunctional and self-defeating behavior.

Managing human beings and their work demands a wide range of skills, insights, and talents. None of us possesses them all. Neither men nor women are genetically or emotionally better suited for the job. Rather, balanced, mature, and self-aware men and women are better able to conquer the stress of the job and eternal struggle for self-management.

Self-management is a big subject and I will not attempt an expansive exploration. Over many years, focusing on my own performance and that of my colleagues, I came to believe certain self-management challenges were among the most relevant indicators of whether we were performing effectively. They are not the only elements of managing ourselves that challenge us throughout our lives but, from the perspective of those we attempt to manage, they matter a great deal.

The Control Dilemma

Avoid Becoming a Pain in the Ass

Few things in life scare us as much as feeling things are out of our control. We are all more at ease when we sense rightly or erroneously we have some leverage over the situation and events before us.

I suspect the dread we have lost or surrendered control lies at the heart of many people's fear of flying. Once we climb into that cabin and the door closes, our fate is in the hands of total strangers in the cockpit. We know statistically, driving is significantly more dangerous but, behind the wheel, we are in control. For me, I felt much the same sense of fear when I handed our teenage children the car keys at 16 pretending it was no big deal.

As managers, our profession demands we exercise some control. Getting to be the boss is what draws many to seek a manager's job. Managers are supposed to provide direction, assign tasks and roles, define behavioral norms, evaluate others, make pay decisions and mediate and resolve conflicts. That's a lot of controlling.

If we provide too little direction and guidance as managers, our employees will feel uncertain and anxious. They have learned from childhood what to expect from authority figures and get angry when we let them down and cause them emotional distress.

If we over-control as managers, micro-manage in other words, they will also get angry and resentful. They will complain among themselves, underperform, or seek employment elsewhere.

Managing our need for control is a balancing act, an endless series of judgment calls with the certain knowledge we will get it wrong from time to time. Picture the bad managers you have experienced. Chances are some of the worst are those who could not surrender control. The best managers are those who learn to maintain the appropriate balance between holding on and letting go. I will have more to say about this balancing act in a later section of this book.

When to Act

Now or Perhaps Never

Deciding when to act, especially in important situations where the stakes of our decisions are high, is stressful, complicated, and often involves highly uncertain risk-reward calculations. No wonder many of us are prone to procrastinate, to think and re-think these decisions, sometimes to the point of exhaustion.

Essentially, it does not matter whether our consequential actions are of a professional or private nature. When you consider the mental and emotional toll difficult decisions can have, there is little difference between a difficult business decision and, deciding when to get married, change jobs, or retire. The temptation to procrastinate is equally powerful.

What is the best way to make a decision to act? As a young man, I thought the answer was clear. You think hard about the decision, weigh carefully the pros and cons, and when the pros have the advantage, you have your choice.

Over the years, I have come to realize it is rarely that simple. There are often so many factors in play that even the task of listing pros and cons frequently produces a seriously inadequate list.

There often comes a moment when a powerful, almost overwhelming feeling tells us NOW is the time to act. It is a moment that renders the issue of acting a matter of feelings and emotions rather than conscious thought. Once this feeling moment passes and our cognitive processes take over, the impetus for action can recede almost indefinitely.

What is working modern neuroscience tells us, is our emotions represent real wisdom. It is in our emotional brain where dopamine neurons, the molecular source of our feelings, continually collect and catalog everything we experience. Drawing on this vast repository of data, the algorithm we call our emotional brain is able to make predictions concerning events and signal us it is time to act. Even when we make mistakes or experience new or unexpected things, our emotional brain simply updates its algorithm and moves on. In essence, our emotional brain is a perpetual learning organism.

Experienced drivers will tell you they knew another driver was about to cut them off split seconds before it happened. How did they know before they consciously had time to process it? It was their emotional brain at work; some subtle thing unconsciously perceived signaled them to hit the brake.

This does not mean we should only consider our emotions or feelings in making decisions. Because something can fool and trick our emotional brain, our conscious reasoning capacity matters. The ability to consider and balance both what our emotional brain is telling us and what our conscious thought process suggests, is the essence of good decision making.

Over-thinking matters is also a bad idea. Some individuals, who have come to deeply trust their ability to logically reason through the elements of any difficult decision, are wary of trusting their feelings. They ignore them. Yet neuroscience suggests our emotional brain is far wiser and better informed than we think and frequently the better indicator of what we should do.

Forethought

Knowing Where You're Going

Blessed with enough time to think before you take some action, a little strategic forethought is a great piece of self-management. Over the years, I developed my own strategy for doing just that. It consists of three simple parts.

WTPIC stands for what are the pieces I control. Is this something I should handle and if so, how? If you answer yes, it should be with deliberate thought. The pieces you always control are if, where, when and how you act.

We frequently inherit problems better left for others to address. Upon reflection, you might consider some issues above your pay level and rank. Perhaps an employee has passed along their problem hoping you will take the time to resolve it for them. Not everything needs confronting at once, especially if the situation has generated strong emotions. When there is a danger you may say or do something you will later regret, a delayed reaction is a worthy choice.

Next comes *CI,* or *commander's intent.* If you intend to act, what is your ultimate objective? Although this sounds so bloody simple, we often swing into action without clarity regarding where we intend to end up.

Say your boss is about to make a decision you think will be a mistake and believe will result in some negative consequences. You have decided to discuss the decision with them. What is your commander's intent? Do you aim to change her mind? Is your purpose to gain some insight into her thinking so you understand the decision more completely? Is your intent to make certain she is fully aware of potential negative outcomes and aims to develop some mitigating strategies? Alternatively, perhaps you want all the above. Each of these intentions will require a different approach to your conversation.

Acting without ultimate goal clarity renders us living examples of the saying "if you don't know where you're going, how will you know if you ever get there?"

Finally, most actions will involve some form of communication, oral or written. *FFS* stands for *first few sentences*. Decades of research findings in the field of communication have found the opening sentences of important discussions strongly correlate with goal attainment.

As a good topic sentence sets a powerful tone for a paragraph, the first few sentences of an important communication or conversation set a tone and convey a definite message about what is to follow. A poor opening, risks creating confusion regarding the message you intend.

Carefully considered, clear, and simple initial sentences are the equivalent of any chess master's opening moves in establishing a direction for the game and imposing his or her will on the process. For this reason I am a big fan of rehearsing your openings if the communication is important. If uncertain, try out your potential opening on somebody else and see how they respond.

I have found that settling on an opening for an important communication is more difficult than I am making it sound. Getting this part right is worth the effort and the results.

Being Accountable

You Did This, So Own It

On November 22, 1968, Japan Airlines Flight 2, was scheduled to land at San Francisco International airport. In heavy fog, its Captain, Kohei Asoh, not adequately trained on the plane's new flight director, landed his aircraft in San Francisco Bay two and a half miles short of the runway.

Fortunately, none of the plane's passengers or crew died. Not long after the incident, the National Transportation Safety Board (NTSB) and Japan Airlines held a press conference attended by reporters and a bevy of lawyers anxious to hear what many suspected would be the usual finger-pointing, who's to blame exercise. The first witness was Captain Asoh and the first question put to him was simply "how did this happen?" As cameras flashed, the Captain spoke: *Asoh fuck up* is all he said. His audience reportedly looked on in shock as they realized that suddenly there were few questions left for anybody to ask.

Author Jerry Harvey's book *The Abilene Paradox* [6] dedicates chapter 5, entitled *Captain Asoh and the Concept of Grace* to this remarkably honest acceptance of responsibility. Harvey called the Captain's three-word response *the Asoh defense* and its candor remains a staple of management consulting advice.

We find a similar striking example of accepting responsibility in a *New Yorker* article entitled *The Fifty-Nine Story Crisis*.[7] The story chronicles the potentially career-ending response of William LeMessurier, one of America's leading structural engineers, when he discovered the supports he designed for the skyscraper-like Citicorp Center in Manhattan were potentially flawed and might not survive the city's occasional high windstorms. LeMessurier blew the whistle on himself and convinced his bosses and Citicorp to reinforce the supports despite the expense, which ran into the millions.

That these stories remain so memorable says a great deal about how much we admire the honest acceptance of responsibility. They likewise remind us how disappointed, frustrated, and angry we feel when we see so many trying to avoid it.

---

6   Jerry B. Harvey, *The Abilene Paradox*, (New York: Jossey-Bass Publishers, 1988).

7   *The New Yorker*, May 25, 1995. 45-53.

Few subjects generate more heated discussion among a workforce than the absence of accountability for mistakes, bad decisions, and flagrant disobedience. Moreover, workplaces where responsibility is routinely dodged never change overnight. Rather they evolve. They evolve because a critical mass of individuals start behaving in ways that challenge an old norm until their behavior eventually becomes the new norm.

We often underestimate how much influence, for good or ill, our behavior has on those who observe us. As designated authorities managers, in particular, are powerful role models for those around them.

The best managers know the importance of being accountable for their actions and act accordingly. They understand a lack of accountability displayed by others is never a sufficient excuse to justify similar behavior. They understand accountability must always begin with us.

Expressing Anger

Scary Monsters Make Bad Managers

To manage other human beings for any length of time guarantees you will occasionally experience angry and negative emotions. When you do, it is a sure sign something or someone is getting the best of you and a good time to take stock and identify who or what exactly it is.

Thinking your way through this can prove simple or difficult. The obvious is often not very clear at all, although perhaps hiding in plain sight. Sometimes we unconsciously try hard to avoid acknowledging the real problem because confronting it directly portends difficulty, time-consuming hard work, and emotional distress. However, anger will not abate for long if we continue to avoid its root cause.

It is helpful at times to talk things through with a colleague, friend, or trusted other. Often they seem to see things more clearly than we do. Moreover, their sustained support can help bolster the confidence we need to tackle the real problem head-on.

Suffering in silence, on the other hand, or pretending you are actually not angry is foolish, self-defeating, and potentially physically harmful. Moreover, if your anger is legitimate, somebody needs to hear about it and learn something.

I have known many managers who pride themselves for letting things roll off their back. However, let us look at what actually happens.

Imagine that each day as you head to work you don an invisible backpack ideally designed for holding unexpressed thoughts, feelings and emotions. Rather than express how you actually feel, you simply reach around and deposit that emotion in your pack. Days, weeks, perhaps a month or two passes and the pack has become heavy. There is a lot of pent-up feeling and emotion in there waiting expression.

Then one day something happens or somebody does something that gets under your skin and out the emotion comes. The heavier your emotional backpack behavioral science warns us, the more likely you will act out your anger in an explosion of emotion directed at the wrong target or far exceeding the severity of the event unleashing it.

Anger is a powerful and profoundly human emotion whose cause may be entirely justified. The question is how to appropriately respond.

Some of us are direct and respond almost at once. Others prefer to think carefully and insure a measured response appropriate to the provocation and situation.

Expressions of anger usually make all parties emotionally uncomfortable. It is always wise to make them as productive as possible. Express your anger in close proximity to the behavior or event that triggered it. Never lose sight of the intent of your anger and try to make that clear. Never accuse or suggest you know why someone acted as they did. Ask them to tell you that.

In the end, the psychological, behavioral, and physical consequences of suppressing anger are too great not to overcome the urge. While ideally the intensity of expression should be in keeping with the seriousness and legitimacy of the cause, the important thing about the emotion of anger is to let it out.

Coping With Frustration

Avoiding an Ulcer

Frustration like anger is a powerful emotion but not the same thing. Unlike anger, frustrations for a manager are a by-product of being responsible for outcomes without the ability to fully direct and control all of the moving parts.

You frequently hear a manager say things like: *how often do I have to tell them, wasn't I clear when I said do this, or is there something confusing about the word no?* It is inevitably frustrating for managers when things take so long to accomplish, so many players and perspectives need accommodating, and many of those people a manager needs to get something done do not fall under their direct authority.

As employees, we all knew how to play the game of waiting to see if the boss really meant what they said, or deciding to slow roll hoping the boss would move on before we had to comply with some decision we opposed.

Tightly woven into a manager's job is the need to revisit things multiple times with many employees and it is frustrating. It takes persistence in the face of frustration to see things through to completion. Moreover, the best managers also understand that giving ill-considered expression to their natural frustrations is generally counterproductive and often leads to more resistance not less.

Frustration builds over time and finds its own home in the emotional backpack. The more we find ourselves overwhelmed with such feelings, the more frustrated we are likely to become and the harder it becomes to think clearly, logically, and productively about the other aspects of our job.

In addition, when frustrated, the more likely it is that we will give vent to our feelings in ways we will come to regret. Some things said and done can never be unsaid or completely undone.

Managing your frustrations, like your anger, is a critical part of managing effectively. Through experience, I discovered four proactive initiatives were helpful in dissipating the frustration-based emotional tension often leading to regrettable reactions.

First, let folks know you are frustrated before real anger sets in. It is perfectly reasonable to explain to somebody how their non-compliance or lack of cooperation is making you feel. The mere expression of your feelings dissipates some of the accompanying emotion.

Second, watch your language. The more frustrated you feel, the more likely a torrent of inappropriate language is likely to spill from your mouth. Over-the-top language obscures your real message and usually elicits an angry response. Use strong, unambiguous language to make your point, but use a measured tone in its expression.

Third, if you must keep reminding someone about the need to do or accomplish something, it is time to make clear that there will be consequences for continued non-compliance. Reminding folks to do what is necessary cannot go on forever.

Finally, once you have indicated that there will be consequences, you must follow through. Otherwise, your authority will mean little to an employee and all those who are watching. Few things get everybody's attention faster than the boss following through on what they said they would do.

Difficult Conversations

Skip the Sugar Coating

There are times when I am convinced avoiding difficult conversations, especially those likely to produce raw emotions, is genetically wired into many of us. Conflict avoidance is among the most frequent shortcomings of even the best managers.

As a manager, engaging in such conversations is part of the job. Withholdings information and honest feedback with the potential to help someone grow, change their behavior, or improve their performance is a cop-out.

Over time, most managers come to appreciate the importance of facing difficult conversations head on. If they do not naturally possess the skills that make these conversations easier, they acquire them. In addition, wise managers frequently remind themselves that necessary discussions verbally avoided, are invariably acted out behaviorally.

The unknown is always how precisely the receiver will respond to your messages and feedback. Fear of an emotional, confrontational response is what underlies a great deal of conflict avoidance behavior. Consequently, managers must learn to trust they can express themselves honestly, both intellectually and emotionally, and successfully cope with the reactions that occur.

The key is to phrase your opening remarks in a way that communicates you recognize there is always another side to things, you have assumed nothing entirely, and you are open to considering what you will hear before passing judgment. You might begin with a brief synopsis of what you have observed, heard, or experienced and invite a response or explanation with an open-ended question; *tell me what happened; why did you respond as you did; how did you read the situation?*

Being able to offer some explanation in a reasonably non-emotional and non-defensive way invites someone to join you in a dialog from which both of you stand to learn something. Your goal is acknowledgment, understanding, acceptance, and action regardless of your message or criticism.

Do not avoid getting to the subject in your opening comments by engaging in meaningless small talk. Although that may make you temporarily more comfortable, it only confuses matters and leaves the other person wondering what this discussion is really all about.

If you get an angry emotional response, stay calm, remain on message and allow for a legitimate expression of emotion from the other side. If necessary, call time out and allow for a cooling off period before revisiting the subject. Above all, never argue with emotion. Emotions are not susceptible to logical reasoning.

Dealing with conflict in the workplace is never easy. However, conflict avoidance is dangerous and threatening to the successful execution of key managerial roles. The best managers are unwilling to run such risks.

New Ideas and Criticism

A Closed Mind Is a Sad Thing

Individually we are never the smartest person in the room. Many brains are better than one, a good idea is a good idea whether it's ours or not, and what we don't know often gets us into trouble.

In a September 23, 2011 *BusinessWeek* article entitled *Ten Things Only Bad Managers Say,* its author Liz Ryan includes a few common pronouncements likely to convince others you are probably not an open minded manager:

- ❖ "I don't pay you to think."

- ❖ "I'll take it under advisement."

- ❖ "Don't bring me problems. Bring me solutions."

- ❖ "Who gave you permission to do that?"

Each of these statements is a notorious wet blanket.

Idea women and men tend to gravitate to managers who are idea generators themselves. Serving as role models, these managers encourage idea sharing by freely sharing their ideas, while never falling in love with them. They encourage others to comment on their ideas, modify and develop them, and they willingly reject their own ideas failing the giggle test. These managers openly admit when someone else has a better idea. As role models, they set the standard for what they want from others and encourage them to follow their lead.

Fear inhibits many of us from engaging in free, innovative, and creative thinking among our colleagues and in front of authority figures. We fear having someone judge us silly or stupid. Good managers create opportunities to let loose one's ideas and ensure they are non-judgmental and safe.

The same welcoming principle applies to criticism. All managers receive some, like it or not. The issue is one's ability to effectively invite and process constructive criticism and modify their behavior accordingly.

Managers who are

❖ Overly sensitive,

❖ Thin-skinned,

❖ Defensive,

❖ Always wanting to palm blame off on somebody else, or

❖ Insistent in the face of all evidence to the contrary, they were not wrong or at fault,

do not invite the constructive criticism of their performance that can help them improve. While they may successfully reduce the volume of criticism they receive, they also render themselves learning disabled with direct consequence for those they manage.

Throughout our professional careers, well-meaning colleagues, friends, and those we currently call our bosses give us plenty of casual advice. In most cases, the stakes involved in heeding or not heeding this type of advice are relatively small. Not a great deal will change one way or another and the advice givers are unlikely to invest much emotional energy in our response.

There are those occasions, however, when we receive feedback or perhaps a potentially career-changing dose of advice carrying significant implications. It can come from a boss, mentor, colleague, or friend.

Perhaps the advice involves a significant career move you should or should not take. Perhaps you are about to authorize some action that will have wide-ranging potential consequences and others will doubt its wisdom. Often this sort of advice will involve something about your performance or operating style someone believes is about to damage your career in some way.

Whatever the nature of this advice, choosing to heed or not heed it is often a complicated psychological and emotional challenge, especially if heeding it involves a tacit acknowledgment of some personal imperfection or the need for change. Your physician informing you your unhealthy life style and poor physical condition needs immediate alteration is easily interpreted as an insult; how could you let yourself go like this. Far to many ignore this sort of advice to their detriment.

How does one remain open to recognizing, hearing, rationally considering, and acting upon relevant criticism and advice? We do so by exercising the self-management discipline required to do the following.

First, listen, do not argue, with what you hear. Turning our immediate attention to alternative ways of looking at the situation, can deny us the benefit of fully recognizing the importance of accurately hearing and considering everything the advice giver has to say.

I can think of no single time in my career when I received this sort of intervention, when the insight rendered into my performance and me was not spot-on, like it or not. There is no such thing as a good manager who cannot look at themselves honestly at important times in their career. The job is simply too hard, and we are simply encumbered by too many weaknesses, to believe that we will always get it right.

Second, take the long view. While some feedback and advice is difficult to absorb and act upon in the short run, the long-term benefits are often the true payoff. Focusing on the eventual goal and reminding yourself regularly of its value helps sustain commitment during the difficult task of any adaptive behavior involved.

Finally, remember that it is in your interest to be adaptable, not stubborn. As simple as this last point sounds, recalling your own life experience offers plenty of examples of individuals who stubbornly refused to adapt or change and suffered the consequences. Self-interest is a very powerful motivator, so go ahead and be a little selfish.

Yes men and women keep their bosses in the dark, a dangerous place to be when there is so much going on and you haven't the time or energy to keep up. Others define managers by their behavior not by their words, no matter how elegant and well delivered they are. Keep reminding yourself of this when it comes to receiving and responding to the ideas and criticism of others.

The Abilene Paradox

When Apparent Agreement Isn't

Gaining a sense of agreement among colleagues on some form of action feels satisfying. However, is it actually agreement or merely a seductive imagined sense of closure?

In 1981, I had the opportunity to view a training film entitled the *Abilene Paradox*. It featured the concept's author, the late Jerry Harvey, then a professor of psychology at George Washington University.

In part, what made Jerry's presentation so captivating and memorable was his wonderful Texan drawl and dry sense of humor as he explained the concept by telling the story of a Harvey family vacation to Coleman, Texas. I laughed so hard the first time I saw it I had to watch the film again to be certain I completely understood the concept. You can find it still on You Tube.

*Jerry's story involved a dreadfully hot Sunday in Coleman
when he, his wife, and his in-laws piled into a car without air
conditioning, and drove the 52 miles between Coleman and
Abilene. In Abilene, they ate a thoroughly disgusting meal at
a local cafeteria. The trip was his father-in-law's suggestion
and although everyone, including his father-in-law, secretly
thought it was a bad idea, everybody found themselves mouth-
ing their agreement with the plan and off they went. It was not
until a full-blown argument later that evening that they
realized they had actually been in complete silent agreement on
the idea's dubious merit. The father-in-law's explanation for his
fateful suggestion was "I was simply making conversation."*[8]

The Abilene Paradox, as Harvey describes it, is the
inability of contemporary organizations to manage silent
agreement, not their inability to manage the conflict involved in disagreement.[9] Real conflict, Harvey argues, occurs when people have real differences and are willing to
discuss them. In the Abilene Paradox, people quietly agree
on the actions they want to take and then do the opposite
to avoid conflict.[10]

While I could say much more about this topic, I com-
mend Jerry's book and film to you instead. The rich re-
al-world examples Jerry offers beyond his story in the film,
at times boggle the mind.

---

8   See *You Tube. The Abilene Paradox, by Jerry Harvey.*

9   Harvey, op. cit., 17.

10 Ibid., see examples,18.

Believe me, the more you come to understand and think about the Abilene Paradox, the more you will see it all around you. When everybody seems in agreement about doing something, stop for a moment, look at faces and body language, and ask yourself and the group, if necessary, are we on the road to Abilene? Sometimes a manager has to drag disagreement out of a group, anxious to avoid conflict. Rarely as a manager did I find any group in complete agreement on anything.

Establishing Priorities

Stop Wasting Time

For me as a new manager, this was a major short-coming. I wrongly assumed my job was to take on whatever came my way, no matter how trivial compared to the big-ticket items on my plate. I quickly became an inefficient time waster.

Fortunately, I had an eye opening training experience, memories of which remain fresh. The program, developed by the Center for Creative Leadership, was The Looking Glass. It was a three and a half day simulation.

Our task was to run a company called Looking Glass. They assigned each of us positions within the company and gave us a position-specific in-box filled with items to prioritize and then develop a plan of action for the opening of business the next day.

The next day began with the company's president making several big announcements throwing all of our plans into a cocked hat. Over the next two days as we attempted to adapt and run the company the faculty intensely observed us, as did our colleagues.

Day 3 was called the barrel. Each of us sat in the middle of a room with faculty and colleagues arrayed around us. We were not permitted a word. We had to listen to their evaluations and critiques.

It was instructive. It was also, at times painful and embarrassing. In retrospect, I cannot imagine a more helpful early on exposure to the realities of management or to the importance of flexibility when it comes to establishing today's priorities.

Establishing priorities as a manager involves making decisions about where to focus energy in a work world with far too many choices and limited time. Those decisions reflect one's judgment about what matters more at any given moment.

The judgment a manager demonstrates in making priority decisions is a key performance criteria superiors are likely to consider in determining their advancement. While there is no exact formula for getting your priorities right, good managers do at least four important things.

❖ They visit their priority list every day. In the hectic pace of most workplaces, this is essential as unforeseen events constantly change the landscape. Yesterday's priorities may be the wrong ones for today.

❖ They work at being flexible. Many of us have difficulty letting go of some things or leaving something undone. One has only so much energy and quality thinking time per day. Deciding what matters most is your call.

❖ Effective managers learn to say things like no, not now, not my problem, and when I have the time. Simple as this sounds, many managers learn this the hard way.

❖ Finally, good managers learn to carve out some down time. A little distance can do wonders in helping sort out what really matters from the rest on your plate.

In my Management Workshop, I use a scenario confronting participants with a crisis in their organization, coupled with criticism from superiors suggesting they missed seeing it coming. Some participants insist on defending themselves from the criticism before addressing the real priority, the crisis. This insight into human nature illustrates why the priority setting component of self-management is so important.

Getting it Wrong

Living With Acceptable Levels of Failure

Continual success is not an option for a manager. Occasions of failure, mistakes, poor judgment, and just plain bad luck are inevitable.

The feelings that generally accompany mistakes and failures are not pleasant but are survivable. A superior calling you out is embarrassing, especially in ear shot of others, but nobody has ever died from it. I suggest three basic psychological survival rules to follow when you find yourself in the cross hairs for the consequences of a mistake or error in judgment for which you are accountable.

Rule One: Failures and mistakes are not an indication of your personal worth as a human being. Do not allow them to undermine your self-confidence or self-esteem. Some failures and mistakes are a natural by-product of the countless decisions and judgment calls one makes as a manager. Accept this or do not become a manager.

Rule Two: Whatever others may say about your mistakes, this matters far less than what you learn and do because of them. Consider the following story about a young executive and his boss, Tom Watson Jr., then CEO of IBM:

The young executive had made some bad decisions that cost the company several million dollars. Summoned to Watson's office fully expecting dismissal, the young executive said, "I

*suppose after that set of mistakes you will want to fire me."
Watson was said to have replied, "not at all, young man, we
have just spent a couple of million dollars educating you."[11]*

The mistakes we all should worry about are those we keep
making over again.

Rule Three: Failures and mistakes are actually an indication that a manager is doing something. They illustrate one
is willing to push the envelope, try something new in the
service of progress or solving a problem, and are prepared
to be creative and innovative when the old way just isn't
working anymore.

Management Consultant Tom Peters preaches action
and often uses the phrase *fail, fast, frequently.* He, like so
many others, recognizes mistakes and failures are the great
learning laboratory. Perhaps nobody summed this up better than Thomas Edison:

Facing a failure, Edison it is said replied: *I have not
failed. I've just found 10,000 ways that won't work.* When his
factory burned down, with much of his life's work inside,
Edison said: *There is great value in disaster. All our mistakes
are burned up. Thank God we can start anew.*[12] Now that is
a positive attitude!

---

11   Edgar H. Schein , *Organizational Culture and Leadership* (New
York: Jossey-Bass Publishers, 2004) 255.

12 See The Happy Manager .com articles/characteristic-of-leadership.

Does It Matter?

A Critical Question to Ask Yourself Often

When our children were younger, departure day for a family vacation was quite a test for me. Having had many preparatory conversations about the limits of our car's trunk space and having reached what I thought was a consensus on departure time, I was consistently irritated by what seemed the excessively laid back, desultory approach of everybody else to the departure event. As excess baggage continued to pile up in the hallway and the departure time faded in the distance, my mood soured.

My family will tell you the first few hours of the trip were far from pleasant, and I will tell you I was not very pleased with myself either. Then one year, as I stood by the car wondering when we would finally hit the road and what we would be forced to leave behind, the following question flashed through my mind: *what does it matter?* My answer, in the grand scheme of things it did not.

Delaying departure an hour or so had no impact on the vacation. What would not fit into the car, with the exception of my bag, was for others to sort out. This single moment of insight improved our vacation departures considerably and served me well throughout my management career.

Managers regularly confront people's behavior and situations that cause them to ask if some management response is required. Simply asking if it matters and why or why not, saves a great deal of time and unnecessary stress. It helps clarify why we need to act in certain situations and why in others, inaction is the better choice.

Maintaining Focus

What Did You Just Say?

In Michael Lewis' book *The Big Short*, he describes the listening style of character Steve Eisman, thusly:

Eisman had a curious way of listening; he didn't so much listen to what you were saying as subcontract to some remote region of his brain the task of deciding whether whatever you were saying was worth listening to, while his mind went off to play on its own. As a result, he never actually heard what you said to him the first time you said it. If his mental subcontractor detected a level of interest in what you had just said, it raised a signal to the mother ship, which then wheeled around with the most intense focus, 'say that again' he'd say.[13]

An intriguing way of paying attention I admit, but not one to win you many fans among your employees, colleagues, or superiors. When somebody cares enough about something to request a manager's attention, they expect full attention and understanding. That requires focus either immediate or at some mutually agreed upon time convenient to both parties.

---

13   Michael Lewis, *The Big Short* (New York: W. Norton & Company, 2010), Kindle Edition. 139.

Focused listening is not always easy to produce. It requires a disciplined attention span, a discipline with psychological and physiological limits. While estimates of our human capacity for focused attention vary by age and our personal interest in the topic, 20 minutes seems to be about the outer limit for most adults. Throw in the many distractions available in the modern world, computers, smart phones, text messages etc., and we could be talking seconds before our brains drift off course.

In situations where focused listening is important, here are a few suggestions for self-management.

Start by attempting to manage your attention span. Consciously determine to concentrate as long as you can on something you consider a high priority topic or conversation. Paying attention does not happen by accident. It is an act of will. If you lack the essential will power to pay attention, little else will help.

Steve Eisman did not lack will power. According to Lewis, he chose not to pay attention until his subcontractor suggested he should. However *once with intense focus he said -- say that again -- you would, because now Eisman was so obviously listening to you, and as he listened so selectively, you felt flattered.*[14]

Eliminate distractions when it is time to concentrate attention on something or someone important. Get away from your computer. Do not answer your phone. Disregard

14 Ibid.

text messages and tweets. If you have a cluttered desk, move elsewhere. Exercising the will power necessary for focused concentration is hard enough without tempting yourself with appetizing sideshows.

When are you at your best each day? This varies for each of us. Some of us are morning people. Some have a burst of energy mid to late afternoon. Try to identify your peak daily performance hours and, as best you can, concentrate on your most important projects, activities, and critical conversations at that time.

In an article entitled *15 Easy Ways to Work Smarter*,[15] author Stephanie Vozza recommends spending 20% of every workday — 90 minutes of an eight-hour day — on your top priorities and high value activities. The work you ignore during that period she calls strategic procrastination. So why not address your 20% when you are at your best?

Take breaks to recharge your batteries. Our bodies and brains have a way of telling us when it is time for a break. Take it. Do not ignore those signals. Take a walk, outside if you can. Let your mind wander to less weighty matters. Do less important work that requires less intense focused attention. Play for a short time. Take a nap.

Research indicates that a short nap each day can have a powerful restorative affect on mental alertness and concentration. I know many segments of the American work

---

15   *Fast Company*, November 2015.

culture in particular look down on napping. Ignore them if you can.

Perspective and Humor

Learning to Laugh at Life and Yourself

One of my favorite workshop quotes came from a young woman during a discussion about self-management. She was expressing frustration with her tendency to beat herself up over every mistake she made. At the very end of her comments she said this: *sometimes I just need to give myself permission to be human*. To that I said, **AMEN**.

On a walk with a colleague after a long day of workshop facilitation, our conversation wandered to the question of why work was often so stressful. Among the things we considered, three characteristics stand out.

❖ Work is timed. There is always a deadline or two we must meet and in some jobs, many of them on any given day. Result: the stress associated with falling behind.

❖ Work is competitive. No matter how much our work processes involve inter-dependent teamwork, some employees perform better than others. Those who perform at a higher level advance more rapidly and end up making more money. Result: the stress associated with being and remaining competitive.

❖ Work is ego involved. How we perform at work effects how we feel about ourselves. Whether our work involves hard manual labor or exhausting intellectual expenditure, we all love the feeling of a job well done. Result: the stress associated with living up to our own expectations and those of others.

Managing the stress associated with our work requires both perspective and a sense of humor.

Imagine watching yourself in action from high above on a balcony. The idea is to visualize yourself performing as in a play, yet being able to simultaneously view the quality and appropriateness of what you are doing. It is akin to what movie actors are able to do when they view the first screening of their latest performance.

These moments of self-evaluation are not always pleasant. However, they are instructive if we are open to what we see. They help us gain some perspective on ourselves, on our strengths and weaknesses, and on ways to become better versions of ourselves. With perspective, we are better able to avoid making mountains out of molehills and turning a routine problem or challenge into a crisis

Humor is the perfect companion of a healthy perspective and a marvelous anecdote for the daily stress of a job. It allows us to see the silliness in some of our own misguided behavior and the humorous, sometimes ridiculous elements in many work situations. There are few things like genuine laughter when it comes to easing tension and stress.

Humor must occur naturally to be effective and it must flow from the realities of a specific situation. Contrived humor will appear contrived.

Effective humor must do no harm. Attempts at humor at the expense of others — personal, sarcastic put-downs or poking at the weaknesses of others, for example — are hurtful and do more harm than good. They may produce laughter but of the uncomfortable variety.

Directing humor at oneself can likewise have a liberating effect on one's employees. I recall an incident from my Army days where I, in my Captain's uniform, tripped and harmlessly fell flat on my back in a busy airport, in front of a large number of enlisted men and women. I could see the uncertainty in their eyes, laugh at what must have seemed a funny pratfall, or stifle that response. Embarrassed though I felt, I could not resist breaking into laughter myself, as I lay there thinking how ridiculous I must have looked. Suddenly they all were laughing as they helped me up. It was an important lesson as an authority figure I never forgot.

Freud considered humor one of the most sophisticated forms of psychological defense. I have long considered it an indispensable asset for remaining balanced and sane as a manager and a way of constantly reminding ourselves to take our work, not ourselves, seriously.

Without a sense of perspective and humor, a manager is in danger of becoming their employee's worst nightmare: arrogant, learning disabled, and a repeat offender. Work,

like life, has its ridiculous moments. Perspective helps us
see these moments, humor allows us to laugh at them and
move on.

4.

Human Beings

*We were looking for employees
but people showed up instead.*

Anita Roddick, late CEO of *The Body Shop*

I like to begin my workshops by asking manager participants what they think they manage. Their answers come
in many forms.

- ❖ My Organization

- ❖ The Mission

- ❖ A Work Process

- ❖ My Employees

- ❖ Employees

- ❖ The Store

- ❖ On Time Deliveries

- ❖ Customer Satisfaction

There is nothing wrong with any of these answers.
There is accuracy in each. However, none dig deep enough.
Underpinning success in managing any of the above objec-
tives are the **HUMAN BEINGS** doing the work.

Managing is the attempt to organize, instruct, guide,
coach, mentor and motivate a collection of people to accomplish specific tasks and goals. Management when done
appropriately involves surrendering doing certain things
and getting others to do them.

Everything a manager does has a human being involved in some way. Managers ignore this fact at their peril and yet such ignorance is easy. There are many things to distract them.

The work managers oversee is important to others, and poor work has consequences. The work itself can be complex, timed, composed of many moving parts, and filled with deadlines. Managers must confront and resolve resource scarcities, a shallow talent pool, poor bench strength, and an excessive need to depend on others over whom they have little control. Poor performance by others could cost them their jobs.

That is a lot to think about and, we haven't even mentioned the part about organizing, instructing, guiding, and motivating those who actually do the daily work. This is why people often come last or not at all for many managers.

For all the complexities of any manager's job, failure to consider the human element in everything they do usually insures a sub-standard performance all around. The best managers make it a daily priority to spend time thinking about the people needed to get every job done.

If knowing and managing yourself is critical to being an effective manager, so is having a basic understanding and acceptance of human nature in all of its glorious, sometimes maddening, and frequently unpredictable manifestations. What makes people tick, motivates them, enables them to both over or under achieve, and occasionally make it seem like they are deliberately trying to drive you crazy?

Unique though we believe we are, humans tend to behave rather predictably confronted with similar situations. If a manager can predict how most will react to something they do, change, announce, or implement, they will be better prepared to respect a human response and think creatively about helping people adjust.

Humans and Change

We Don't Easily

Humans in general dislike change. They find the uncertainty involved in the unknown unsettling, anxiety producing and occasionally a source of fear.

Psychiatrist Harry Levinson once reminded a group of us at his leadership seminar that all change, large or small, involves loss, and it is in our nature to mourn and lament these losses before full acceptance becomes possible. As the author of some change, what a manager sees from many of those affected may differ from person to person but in the aggregate, it will likely look like resistance. The speed with which each individual comes round to embrace the change will vary.

To deny individuals some time to make change adjustments is disrespectful. To let resistance continue indefinitely is bad management. You must make the judgment call regarding when it is time to move on. Helping people work through their feelings regarding change always helps and demonstrates human understanding. It helps to gradually assist others to see what gains the change represents, not just what is being lost.

It is likewise in our nature to test whether a change is real and whether someone means what they say. We begin exercising this inherent testing early in our lives.

During a visit with our daughter and her family some years ago, I had the opportunity to witness human nature in all its glory. The situation involved our daughter's son Max, then almost 2 years old, and his mother. Max was the proud owner of a wooden train set: engine, cars, tracks, bridges, buildings, etc. A little destructiveness from Max and it easily became a jumble. This day Max had a mind to be rough and mom expressed an emphatic no. So here was Max and his mother locked in a test of wills as I stood by and tried hard not to laugh. The outcome seemed all too obvious to an experienced parent.

With their eyes locked on each other, Max pushed the train engine forward with vigor disrupting a few tracks and mom articulated another firm no. Another push by Max elicited an even more emphatic no. At this point had Max understood the three strikes and your out rule, he might have quit. However, one last vigorous push and mom was on her feet, collecting parts for secreting away. Max was in tears having realized that this time no actually did mean no.

You can count on it. Try to change something and some, if not all of those affected, will test its permanence. It's a negotiation process designed to test flexibility and find out whatever wiggle room there is in the change's implementation. Anticipating the test helps one prepare an appropriate response, one reinforcing the message that this change is real and requires eventual acceptance.

Finally, lack of consequences for continued resistance, sabotage, or passive aggression authorizes them all. Try as you might to help others adjust to the demands of change, there are those whose resistance seems limitless. Eventually there is only one appropriate response to such behavior. The bus is departing tomorrow morning you inform them. Time to decide if you will be on the bus or not.

Failure to address excessive resistance or sabotage is not only authorizing, it suggests its efficacy to others. Enough ignored resistance is often sufficient to undermine any change, and it is all too human to take advantage of such authorization.

When you appropriately address resistance, it sends a powerful message that the time has come for making peace with the change and move on. It is characteristic of most of us to learn from the consequences of pushing too far.

You Can't Fix People

But Sometimes We Try

The urge to fix people is one of the most common areas where managers venture into dangerous and usually fruitless territory.   We are often uncertain regarding what is best for ourselves, let alone what is best for others.

The best managers are always prepared to provide advice and counsel assisting others down the path towards solving a problem or meeting a challenge. They assiduously avoid prescribing a solution. While it is difficult to watch somebody else struggle with a problem, listening, understanding, and providing encouragement will serve them better than a misguided effort to impose a fix.

There are a series of dramatic and powerful scenes in the movie *When a Man Loves a Woman*. A wife, played by Meg Ryan, has just returned from an alcoholic rehab program and is struggling to work through the road ahead with her airline pilot husband played by Andy Garcia.

During years of his wife's alcoholic binges, Andy's character has had to frequently pick up the pieces, cover for her missteps, and struggle to hold the family together. That role has given him a sense of value, and he has done his level best as a family provider and loving husband to fix things. Post rehab, it is the last thing his wife needs him to do. How angry and frustrated he feels when his wife informs him that every time he attempts to fix things and clean up a mess it only makes her feel more worthless, less capable of coping, and depressed. She must now find her own way to emotional health even if it means an end to their marriage.

The painful point of the story is people must fix themselves, regardless of the well meaning, loving attempts of others to do it for them. It is instructive, in this regard, to view how Andy Garcia's character copes with his challenge. It is a wonderful example of self-management.

All of us who have managed can probably recall a time when we felt an irresistible urge to jump right into someone else's problem. Perhaps, based upon our own experience, we felt confident we knew what was best. The hard truth remains that our views will represent a potential fix, only if someone else is willing to adopt our advice as their own.

I believe every manager can play an important role in helping an employee, colleague, or superior cope with some difficult challenge. A good place to begin is helping someone acknowledge, confront, and own the challenge they face.

A manager's organizational knowledge can also be valuable in providing a road map of steps, sources of assistance, and other resources available. Here it is important to avoid the temptation to prescribe rather than provide a menu of choices and options.

Finally, remembering Rome wasn't built in a day, demonstrating patience and showing support for someone actively addressing a problem can provide vital encouragement, especially when the process will be a lengthy and difficult one. Such support is a sign of confidence their efforts will succeed and can make a big difference.

They Are Adults

Treat Them Accordingly

Do those entrusted to your management ability work for, with, or under you? Not long ago, I interviewed a retired manager. When I asked her how she would like her former employees to describe her, she replied, "I hope they would say they enjoyed working for and with me, not under me." As I pondered her response, I became aware of how subtle the differences were between these three prepositions and how much difference they could make in terms of performance, morale, team cohesiveness, motivation, creativity, initiative, and out put.

In a hierarchical organization, all employees work under some manager's authority. Employees understand this. However, the term under carries some negative weight, a sense of being burdened down, of being on some sub-level, of not being of equal class or status. Our associations with this notion generally imply a subservient power relationship and are not entirely pleasant.

Working for someone conveys a slightly more pleasing connotation. While our employee status is still implied, it somehow seems less onerous than being under someone's thumb. Working for someone does not imply a partnership but it does make the possibility of achieving that sort of working relationship seem more plausible.

Working with someone comes closest to the idea of a partnership. It implies a collaborative endeavor where all parties have a roughly equal say, the right to say no, the notion decisions will be the result of discussion and negotiation, and that consensual agreement on direction will often replace following an order.

Here we are admittedly dealing with semantics. All employees come under some bosses authority. Much about work in modern organizations resembles the parent-child paradigm. Take for example the annual Performance Appraisal.

Consultant and author Peter Block describes these appraisals as fundamentally an instrument for exercising control. "You can soften them all you want," he writes, "call them development discussions, have them on a regular basis, have the employee identify the improvement areas instead of the boss, and discuss values. None of this changes the basic transaction. If the intent of the appraisal is learning," says Block, "it is not likely to happen when the context is evaluation and judgment." [16]

16   Peter Block, *Stewardship*, (San Francisco: Barrett-Koehler Publishers, 1993), 152.

Although performance reviews are part of every manager's job, they are not how adults usually interact. If you doubt this, try to imagine giving your partner in life a formal annual appraisal of their performance as your wife, husband, or significant other.

Nothing prevents a manager from trying to avoid as many boss/employee interactions as possible. This is what I believe my manager interviewee was implying. She was describing the ideal as a working environment where a collection of adults, day to day so to speak, felt they were working together as partners toward their common goals.

All managers have considerable power to shape, positively or negatively, the nature of the day-to-day relationships they have. While no manager can escape the de-facto, unequal quality of the power relationship that exists, they can lessen the occasions when they need to remind an employee of who is in charge, or exercise their power to order compliance.

The best managers understand when people are working collaboratively, each fulfilling their designated role and each contributing their fair share of ideas and input to a collective goal, they unleash the spirit of initiative, creativity, and passion leading to high quality performance. Paradoxically, the more power over others a manager surrenders, the more power they gain through others to move their organization forward.

Behavior or language directed at adults implying ownership will eventually spark resentment and resistance. Implying you own adults is not a blueprint for success as a manager.

Safety and Trust

A Foundation for Performance

In his book *Smarter, Faster Better*[17] author Charles Duhigg's second chapter is entitled *Teams: Psychological Safety at Google and Saturday Night Live.* In this chapter, Duhigg discusses the process through which groups and teams develop behavioral norms. These are the traditional understandings, acceptable behaviors, and unwritten rules — often quietly understood rather than openly expressed or codified — that govern how we behave in group settings and undertakings.

The creation of behavioral norms is a universal human activity and it would be almost impossible for us to function effectively in collectives without them. Group norms determine which of our behaviors are acceptable and which are not when we are acting in a group.

Fans of the original Saturday Night Live cast will find fascinating Duhigg's description of how these highly talented, intense, and extremely competitive men and women

---

17 Charles Duhigg, *Smarter Faster, Better* (New York: Random House, 2016).

managed under the guidance of Director Lorne Michaels to successfully pull off one fantastically funny team skit after another. Their secret was each of them felt safe to be themselves and trusted in each other's support. [18]

Duhigg also focuses attention on a Google project code named *Aristotle*, conducted by members of its People Analytics Group. Their task was to determine what factors were most likely to improve the effectiveness of Google's various teams. Their answer was the right group norms.

When Laszlo Bock, head of Google's People Operations Department (Google's HR), addressed Google employees assembled in their auditorium and via video screens, he presented a series of slides and told them that Project Aristotle had concluded five key norms seemed to matter most.

Teams need to believe that their work is important; teams need to feel their work is personally meaningful; teams need clear goals and defined roles; team members need to know they can depend on one another; but most important, teams need psychological safety. [19]

Human history amply illustrates man is by nature a social animal. Throughout life, we regularly engage in activities demanding cooperation and interdependence for successful accomplishment. Talent, innate abilities, and natural aptitudes are critical elements and go a long way

18   Ibid., 51-56.
19   Ibid., 65-66.

toward predicting a team's potential for success, but they are rarely enough. Without agreed upon behavioral norms, trust in one another, and a feeling that we are psychologically safe in each other's company, the prospect for effective teamwork fades.

In sports, how often have we seen a team loaded with talent fail to produce the team chemistry necessary to fulfill their potential? Chemistry invariably comes down to a set of basic human needs whose fulfillment we all crave in the collective endeavors marking our lives.

I recently heard a story about the teller's supervisor who initiated an employee opinion survey designed to identify what the staff thought of his performance. The supervisor promised the responses would be anonymous and had arranged to have another staff member filter out identities before he reviewed a summary of the results.

Over a weekend, the supervisor spied the completed surveys stacked on the staff member's desk and could not resist a quick peek. Angered by some critical performance feedback, this boss knew exactly who had said what because the identities had not yet been removed. According to the storyteller, this supervisor subsequently displayed no intention of acting on any of the feedback critical or otherwise, and showed signs of bearing a grudge against those who had been critical of him.

Consider the act of asking somebody for feedback as an unstated but implied contract: you tell me what you think and I will listen respectively and respond appropriately. Fulfilling this contract is a sign of respect. Refusing to acknowledge or act on the feedback makes others feel like they are being jerked around.

How candid are the employees of the above supervisor likely to be in the future? How trusting and secure would most of us feel in such an environment? This supervisor has probably been cut off from important lines of communication, damaged morale, and mortgaged their potential as a leader.

Consider some of the possible negative interpretations the above supervisor's behavior might create:

❖ He is a phony who only wishes to appear that he wants feedback;

❖ He is insecure, immature and can not handle an honest critical response;

❖ He is deceitful and asked for feedback simply to identify, and act against, those who might see some fault in him.

None of these interpretations is very flattering and none will enhance a manager's ability to do their job.

Safety and trust in a working environment depend upon a boss's reputation for telling the truth. I am not referring to avoiding the big lie. Only the most foolish managers would, claim a college degree they did not earn, steal from their company and attempt to lie about it, or promise an employee something they could not possibly deliver.

Countless managers, however, shade the truth about a great many things. In an effort to put a positive gloss on reality, perhaps a manager emphasizes only what serves that purpose, or they fail to communicate certain facts a more balanced presentation would require. Telling the truth amounts to leveling with people on a consistent basis.

One of my favorite passages in the Harry Potter series occurs in book four, *Harry Potter and the Goblet of Fire.* The Dark Lord Voldemort has returned and murdered a student at the Hogwarts School for Wizards. Headmaster Albus Dumbledore is about to address the student body and provide some explanation of events.

Cedric Diggory was murdered by Lord Valdemar," he announces. "The Ministry of Magic does not wish me to tell you this. It is possible that some of your parents will be horrified that I have done so, either because they will not believe that Lord Voldemort has returned or because they think I should not tell you so, young as you are. It is my belief, however, that the truth is generally preferable to lies, and that any attempt to pretend that Cedric died as a result of an accident, or some sort of blunder of his own, is an insult to his memory.[20]

20   JK Rowling, *Harry Potter and the Goblet of Fire* , 722.

Most of us admire those we know who are unafraid to tell the hard truth. We recognize the inherent respect for others contained in the act of frankness. We appreciate the absence of spin when it comes to sharing the facts with adults so that they know exactly what they are facing.

It is not about being blunt or harsh. Nor does frankness require a lack of feeling or empathy. Rather it is about the facts pleasant or unpleasant and the belief that others are best able to cope when given the true story.

Many of my readers have undoubtedly sat in closed rooms and heard the phrase *for this room only*. When you hear this phrase, consider the following two things. It is likely that many outside the room already know whatever it is, so who is fooling whom? Moreover, if a workforce actually knows something is afoot but not the facts, they will engage in a vigorous round of making things up — overwhelmingly negative things — which will become the hallway rumors of the day.

A manager who consistently provides the straight skinny creates an environment where trust and a sense of psychological security are possible. Being glib and eloquent is great. Being straight with those you manage is even better.

Expectations

Determine Outcomes

Behavioral science research has consistently demonstrated that the vast majority of human beings will endeavor to live up to or down to the expectations, they believe others have of them. My own experience has been that the ability of managers to help set and support realistic expectations for those entrusted to them is perhaps their most powerful motivational tool.

Benjamin Zander's website describes him as a conductor, teacher, and dynamic world-traveling speaker on management and leadership issues. While I have never had the pleasure of attending one of Mr. Zander's leadership talks, I have had the opportunity of hearing his unique and provocative views on film and on-line. One of Zander's most frequent messages concerns the power of people *having possibilities to live into*.

I frequently raise this topic in my management workshops and participants quickly draw the parallel between expectations and possibilities to live into. Although similar, they are not the same.

In the world of work, those in charge generally present us with their expectations concerning our performance. These expectations are an important component of good management practice, they provide motivational goals and targets, and they provide us with an understanding of the performance judgment criteria we face from our superiors.

We have grown accustomed to working in an expectations-centered environment, thanks to our parents, guardians, families, teachers, clergy, etc. Many of us would be lost without a sense of what is expected of us.

I am not about to suggest managers abandon the use of performance expectations. Rather, I am suggesting the enhanced potential power of helping employees transform imposed expectations into self-defined possibilities they are willing to pursue.

The key difference between these two concepts lies in the role played by the individual to whom the possibility applies. While expectations are generally external standards to be met, a possibility presents the individual with considerably more control over determining the criteria for achieving an agreed upon goal. Consider the following example:

Benjamin Zander was teaching a graduate class at the New England Conservatory. He had a collection of nervous, high strung, highly competitive students to instruct. His dilemma was how to make them relax and learn. At his wife Rosamund's suggestion, he decided to give everyone an A from the beginning of the year. There was one condition. At the end of the year, each participant had to submit a personal letter explaining what they believed they had accomplished to warrant their A.[21]

The result was a shift in attitude, a shift that made it possible for the students to speak freely about their thoughts, feelings and dreams, while also supporting their classmates in pursuit of their dreams. For the Zander's it transported students from the world of measurement into the universe of possibility. The A became a possibility to live into, not a standard to live up to.[22]

What struck me at once about this switch in paradigms was the power it gives all of us to become an additional judge of our own performance. It is an opportunity to ensure our goals, though perhaps a stretch, are realistic and achievable.

I have known so many individuals over the years who are painfully dependent on what others think of their efforts and feel constantly burdened by the fear they are not living up to someone else's expectations. Once trapped in this dependency, it is difficult to break free.

Some will say the Zander's are wrong; we must earn our A, not have it given to us as a free good. However, managers do not judge workplace performance via test scores, exams, and scholastic grades. At work, the goal of effective management is to find ways to assist every em-

21 Rosamund and Benjamin Zander, *The Art of Possibility* (New York: Penguin Books, 2002), *25-53.*

22 Ibid., 26.

ployee to achieve their maximum potential. It is in the service of this objective, that helping employees shape possibilities for themselves has its greatest potential power.

While a manager's expectations will always matter to employees, the liberating and motivational challenge of achieving a possibility of one's own design, can often unlock those special talents hidden inside.

In 1968, Harvard Professors Robert Rosenthal and Lenore Jacobson undertook a research project referred to as the Pygmalion Effect[23]. After pre-testing a group of elementary school students on an intelligence test, Rosenthal and Jacobson selected a randomly chosen cross-section (20%) of them and told their teachers all of them had unusual potential for intellectual growth. Re-tested eight months later, all of the randomly selected students the teacher's thought would bloom scored significantly higher on their intelligence tests. The teacher's pre-biased sense of possibilities for these students shaped their teaching efforts which helped make the student's potential a self-fulfilling prophecy.[24]

---

23 Pygmalion, a sculptor of Greek Mythology fame, created a female statue of great beauty. Absent a wife and enamored by the beauty of his own making, he prayed to the goddess Venus for a wife in the statue's likeness. Granting his wish, Venus brought his statue to life.

24 For more details on this research, GOOGLE the Rosenthal Experiment.

It requires skill, empathy, and insight for a manager to discover the individual talents and potential of all those they supervise and to devise a tailored set of positive performance expectations and possibilities designed to stretch, develop, and motivate. There are few greater pleasures for a manager than having the opportunity to sit back and observe a group of talented, motivated, and dedicated human beings strive for and fulfill their performance potential.

Acknowledgment

A Power Tool

There are plenty of marvelous books on management and leadership suggesting the golden rules of being a success. They encompass the big things to do and not do and provide plenty of examples.

The best managers spend time considering the wisdom of what they read and learn in classes and training. They work hard to adapt their management style to the situations they face and cultivate flexibility in the face of constant change. The very best managers are also masters of *the little things.*

The little things are more a matter of intuition and an inherent grasp of human nature than a product of strategic planning, book learning, or deliberate intent. Of all the little things, none is more important than the provision of acknowledgment and affirmation. Hold the door open for someone or do someone a favor and what do we expect? Some form of acknowledgment; a nod of the head, a thank you, some sign of appreciation.

Affirmation that we have done something of value reinforces our sense of worth, suggests we have made some small contribution, and verifies somebody noticed. Small though these signs of acknowledgment often are, when withheld, we experience angry, negative emotions.

Most managers are keen to acknowledge the big contributions their employees make; the killer sale, the grand project success, and the idea that turns into a rainmaker. Yet, every day employees make numerous small contributions collectively keeping things running in the right direction. When they receive no sign of positive reinforcement, it suggests nobody paid attention or gave a fig.

Each day good managers are keen to provide a few pats on the back, a couple of nice jobs, and an occasional well done. To the recipient of these small gestures of acknowledgment, the affirmation they are not just doing their job but doing it well, matters a great deal. They signify their boss is paying attention, values them and their performance, and encourages them to strive for even greater contributions.

Find those managers who people say they love working for and you generally find a manager who pays attention to and acknowledges both the big and the little things.

Untested Assumptions

Your Mortal Enemy

It is so incredibly easy for humans to assume they know things about others without a shred of evidence to support them. So easy, the process is unconscious. We simply feel convinced we know. The problem arises when we act on these assumptions without testing them. The process is so automatic we fail to realize we are in trouble until it is too late.

We are in luck. There is an antidote.

?s

Our ability to ask questions and gather facts can save us a lot of embarrassment and trouble. I will have more to say about the art of asking questions in a moment, but first let's look at why we are so prone to act before we know.

One of my workshop scenarios involves a manager receiving a call from an employee's parents. The call involves criticism of how they are managing their precious child. More than a few of the participants can hardly wait to hang up, descend upon the employee and deliver a tongue lashing for putting their parents up to the call. Does the manager know this is what happened? No, it is an untested assumption for the moment.

Recall my earlier discussion of how our brain works regarding our decisions to act. I described how the dopamine neurons in our emotional mid-brain stimulate feelings based on a current event and instantly signal a course of action predicated upon our past experience.

Unfortunately, our emotional brain can be wrong, fooled and tricked. We can jump to the wrong conclusion about something with no confirming information, or by relying on what turns out to be a pattern-defying random event we misread. Author Malcolm Gladwell argues that because these first impressions or *snap judgments* can serve us for both good and ill, we must take active steps to manage and control them.[25]

Our conscious reasoning capacity matters as much as what our emotional brain is signaling us. A well-balanced blend of reason and feeling is the essence of good decision-making. Because our conscious reasoning and information gathering process is much slower than our emotional brain, patience and reflection are required to test instantaneous impulses before we act.

A good place to begin reflection is considering what psychologists refer to as the confirmation or my-side bias. It represents the human tendency to see what we want or expect to see, and to seek, remember, favor, and interpret information and facts in ways that confirm our pre-existing beliefs and assumptions. Concurrently, we give considerably less attention and credibility to alter-

---

25 Malcolm Gladwell, *Blink* (New York: Little Brown and Company, 2005), 97-98. The case studies in this book provide powerful reinforcement for Gladwell's suggestion that we consciously test our initial impressions.

native possibilities, information interpretations, and outcomes.

There are many strategies for avoiding the confirmation bias but it inexorably comes down to one's ability to confront the idea that we might be wrong. Once we look the prospect of being wrong straight in the eye, we open up our minds to new ways of thinking and new ways of looking at available facts and information. It allows us to ask critical *if not this, then what* questions.

It is Rudyard Kipling who said *I keep six honest serving men they taught me all I knew, their names were what and where and when and how and why and who.* It is Albert Einstein who said *if he had an hour to solve a problem and his life depended on it, he would spend the first fifty-five minutes determining the proper questions to ask.*

A number of years ago, I had the opportunity at a Harvard seminar to hear some of the actual recorded tapes of The Executive Committee (EXCOM) meetings chaired by then President John Kennedy during the terrifying Cuban Missile Crisis. As the world stood on the brink of a nuclear war, the President confronted one untested assumption after another. His articulate and persuasive EXCOM colleagues were full of opinions concerning what the Russians would and would not do in response to US actions. What surprised me most hearing the tapes was how infrequently the President spoke. He listened. When he did speak, it was often in the form of a penetrating question designed to differentiate opinions from fact. If ever there was a time for effective Presidential management of a crisis, that was it and Kennedy's questioning mind served him and his country well.

In the hectic, fast-paced world of modern work, taking time to ask clear, assumption-challenging, objective questions is not always easy. As author Gillian Tett points out, the structure of today's organizations only further complicate matters with their numerous competing sub-organizations (silos) going their own way, jealousy grading their turf, hoarding their information and data, and competing with each other for supremacy and resources. It is a world where countless managers find it difficult to understand many of the events swirling around them, much less ask the correct questions of the correct people allowing them to differentiate the forest from the trees.[26]

Ms. Tett champions our cultivating the anthropologist's ability to look at our inside world as if we were *outsiders looking in.*[27] Such a perspective encourages skepticism concerning the continuing veracity of our mental constructs and of our assumed mental prowess. Then we can begin the questioning process allowing us to reduce our ignorance and test our assumptions.

The best questions are direct, objective, open and probing. They contain a simple vocabulary that leaves little doubt about what we are asking. We are looking for facts

---

26 Gillian Tett, *The Silo Effect* (New York: Simon and Schuster, 2016), 12-18.
27 Ibid., 49.

not opinions no matter how strongly held. Good questions reveal nothing about the questioner's point of view or potential bias and allow the answerer to respond in whatever way they deem best.

Use of direct, probing questions may appear threatening and intimidating to some. Your ability to read the verbal and non-verbal feedback a question generates, and willingness to adjust, will enhance the prospects of realizing your knowledge goal.

Ask the same questions of many people in your organization. Then explore the gap spaces between their answers. Always assume there are important things you should but do not know. Then ponder ways to get at these uncertainties.

When someone in your organization warns you about something others around you dismiss or which does not seem likely to you, do not disregard it. Make those who dismiss the warning defend their reasoning with facts.

Just because you are not expert in everything, do not assume a basic understanding of important parts of your organization is beyond you. Make experts translate their concepts and jargon into plain language any layman can grasp. If they cannot, suspect trouble.

Insist on data as the basis of your decisions. Some really smart people can present their opinions as if they were scientific fact. The best managers dig to see what's beneath the surface of all points of view and are instantly skeptical when one of their important questions elicits a response something like: "no worries boss, everything is fine and under control."

Above all, it is critical to know when to persist with your questions and when to stop. Time constraints for action usually signal a stopping point. Do not allow pursuit of more information to serve as an excuse for putting off unpleasant decisions. The very best questioners usually have a knack for knowing when enough is enough.

Assumption-clarifying thinking is not hard but the search for new information and data often is. If you are intellectually lazy or one of those individuals who never thinks they are wrong about anything, why bother considering alternatives.

Authenticity and Predictability

Being Yourself

Authenticity is one of the most important qualities that create the degree of comfort we seek in our relationship with a managerial superior. Authenticity represents our superior's willingness to consistently be precisely who they are.

I have observed, worked for, and worked with managers representing a broad range of styles. A few of them

I am happy to forget. In most cases, I was able to reach a comfortable accommodation once I was able to figure out what made them tick and would require of me.

The key ingredient the best managers in my experience possessed was their predictability. That is, with a fair degree of reliability, I could count on them to remain essentially the same person from day to day, situation to situation, and event to event.

Predictability simplifies the effort of establishing relationships, interactions, and social networks. Few things are as un-nerving as attempting to engage others whose behavior, responses, and actions can vary significantly, even though the situations may vary little. Especially in a work setting where manager-employee relationships are common, a manager whose actions and reactions are difficult to anticipate becomes an intellectual and emotional challenge.

Individuals I refer to as authentic are those who are sufficiently comfortable in their own skin to remain there. They are individuals at ease with who they are and willing to be themselves whatever the situation. They are not play actors seeking to determine the required role a situation seems to demand, nor are they illusionists hoping to fool others into believing they are something they are not.

Authentic individuals possess a high degree of magnetism. We are drawn to them as bosses. It is not that they are tough or easy-going, brilliant or simply smart, introverts or extroverts, nor is it the precise degree to which we actually like them on an emotional level. Rather it is their authenticity. We can pretty much depend upon the character of their interactions with us and thus calibrate our behavior accordingly.

Being authentic and consistently dependable in your behavior, will not necessarily make you popular with your employees. However, they will respect and appreciate at least that you are the person they have come to expect you to be.

5.

Responsibility

Rank does not confer privilege or power.
It imposes responsibility.

Peter Drucker

It is our choices, Harry, that show what we truly are,
far more than our abilities.

JK Rowling as Professor Dumbeldore in
Harry Potter and the Chamber of Secrets.

There is one moment, whether you apply for the job or somebody offers it to you, when all new mangers say yes to their first assignment. At that moment, very few of us fully comprehended what we are actually agreeing to.

With our yes, we de facto agree to become a designated authority willing to shoulder and exercise responsibility on behalf of our organization. As we soon discover that means facing countless decisions with uncertainty and doubt, discovering the true challenges of managing and leading and realizing there is no longer an upper strata called *them*. We are now them.

All new managers eventually discover responsibility is a heavy, frequently stressful burden. We are accountable for everything we do in the job and much we do depends on the performance of others over whom we have only partial control. We can delegate all we want but in the end, it all comes back to us.

While responsibility never rests easy on a sane man or women's shoulders, it rests easier once a manager comes to grips with the requirements for successfully shouldering and exercising responsibility.

Decisions

They Are Really Acts of Faith

The best decision you can make is the best decision you can make, based on what you know at the time you need to make it. This profound insight came from a 20-something young woman at Saturn Motor Company whose job was head of their car Buy-Back Department.

Managers are required to make decisions, and any manager will make a lot of them big and small. Every day it is one decision after another affecting those they manage in some way or another.

You will make many decisions on tight deadlines, some almost instantaneous, and more often than not without all the facts. It often seems like working a jig saw puzzle minus all the straight edge pieces that help set the boundaries, many of the internal pieces missing, and no box cover telling you what the final product should look like.

The decisions managers make are essentially acts of faith. The situations generally suggest a range of options, each buying something and each with a cost. We must choose. Past experience and gut instincts help but still we must choose. Only after implementing the decision and assessing what happened will we know if we are pleased with the results. Was it the right call regardless of the results?

We will never know. Life does not allow us a peek at what would have happened had we chosen another option.

Fear of making the wrong call or of making a mistake freezes many a manager into inaction, procrastination, or insisting on more time for thinking or considering a few more opinions. This is not the road to management success. Mistakes and wrong calls will happen. What is important is what we do and learn.

In September 2011, the American-based media provider Netflix announced that it planned to raise prices for its services and separate into two companies: a DVD mail order operation called Quikster and an internet streaming service retaining the name Netflix. Customer response was almost immediate and negative. Netflix estimates it lost almost a million customers and watched its share price fall substantially.

In October 2011, Netflix reversed course. In a series of apologies, it admitted its mistake in underestimating the appeal of a single website and service called Netflix, and announced it was abandoning its plan for a Quikster brand. Eighteen months later, *BusinessWeek* chronicled what it called "one of the all-time great comebacks" by Netflix.[28] Was this all due to their apologies and abandonment of Quikster? Probably not, but it is easy to imagine the critical role their rapid reversal played.

---

28 BusinessWeek, May 13, 2013. The Cover Story.

Stories like this illustrate the power and positive impact of acknowledging a mistake and doing so reasonably fast. It quickly disarms most critics. They may still wish to focus on your fallibility but from your perspective, you are now free to engage in what I call a do-over or mulligan. You may have some damage to repair but the faster you get at it and learn the lesson that prevents a repeat performance, the better.

If a rapid acknowledgment of a mistake has such advantages, why do many of us often refuse to do so? I believe this is a very complicated psychological question. Suffice to say the process is challenging. It requires the intellectual and emotional ability to distance ourselves sufficiently from our actions to see the facts for what they are and the maturity to humble ourselves in front of others by admitting we were wrong.

Think of the damage done when an individual refuses to acknowledge a misjudgment or mistake, even in the face of overwhelming evidence to the contrary. Time spent defending a mistake is time wasted. Needed damage control and repair are delayed, while others are forced to witness a painful, immature display of denial. The therapeutic and cathartic effect of rapidly acknowledging a mistake erodes proportional to the length of one's disavowal.

The best managers make a practice of looking reality straight in the eye, acknowledging poor decisions and misjudgments, and turning do-overs into corrective action.

Managing and Leading

Knowing When to Do One or the Other

The word manager is a title. It stipulates that its holder is a designated authority authorized to execute all of the responsibilities assigned to a specific managerial role. Holding the title does not mean the holder is actually managing, or imply the quality of performance. Others will judge the quality of the managing by what they see.

The act of managing generally involves organizing and coordinating the activities of a particular business or organization. The aim is to achieve the organization's defined purpose or mission. It is a straightforward activity involving supervision, assignment decisions, resource allocation, performance evaluation, requirement fulfillment, and customer interaction. Managing is an activity we have grown up to respect as essential to daily living and our organizational lives.

Ronald Heifetz, co-founder of the Center for Public Leadership at the Harvard Kennedy School, provides a slightly different but complementary perspective on managing. As designated authorities, he argues, managers are expected to fulfill the essential social functions of all authority figures:

❖ Direction,

❖ Protection

❖ Orientation to role, status and place

❖ Define and maintain behavioral norms, and

❖ Resolve Conflict.[29]

Executing these functions and other management responsibilities works best when there is a broadly recognized
and accepted way of doing things. There are tried and true
ways to get the job done and solve problems. There is likely
to be little disagreement expressed when a manager issues
an order or asks employees to go about something in a
practiced, widely accepted way, or one that has worked re-
peatedly in the past.

What happens, however, when the tried and true is
no longer working? What happens when there is no obvious fix to a problem? What happens when a manager
decides that some things need to change and a portion of
the workforce intend to resist? What happens when the
way ahead will require learning and new skills? These situations are not subject to simple management functions.
They require leadership or what Heifetz calls *getting people
to do adaptive work.*[30]

29 See Ronald A Heifetz , *Leadership Without Easy Answers* (Boston:
Harvard University Press, 1994), Chapter 3.
30 Ibid., see chapter 4 for a detailed discussion of the anatomy of
adaptive work.

Adaptive, positive work requires a manager to envision an approach representing a new way and change. Leading will require a manager to dedicate herself to driving that change process no matter how hard the task, or long it takes. When a manager decides to lead, employees often respond with considerable anger and resistance because they would rather their boss protect them from the uncertainty of change.

Unlike the term manager, leader is not a title. Organizations have no formal roles called leader, although we often confuse the issue by calling people in high places by that name whether they provide leadership or not. Anyone can become a leader provided they are willing to lead. However, every manager eventually confronts situations requiring leadership on their part; the old way will not work anymore.

Deciding to lead is a conscious choice with all the risks involved. It is about being proactive not reactive. There will be considerable discussion and disagreement among those you wish to lead concerning both the need for change and the correct road ahead. Like all management decisions, leadership involves an act of faith that the new direction is the correct one despite the uncertainties involved.

Management requires skill. Leadership requires courage, initiative, creativity, and guts. Bureaucracy and the chain of command can be constraining but effective leaders look for ways out of boxes and around obstacles. Effective leaders accept the fact that despite their best efforts they might fail, yet they lead anyway.

Below is an example of a single individual exercising both her managerial and leadership skill. I have used it often because I believe it dramatically illustrates the difference between managing and leading and the need for designated authorities to do both.

Consider a hypothetical cardiologist. She is experienced, highly regarded, and excels both in the surgical suite and as a personal physician to her cardiac patients.

In surgery, she is the absolute boss. The procedures she undertakes and directs are precisely the challenges that have a tried and true approach and solution. The anesthesiologists, nurses, and attending staff are well trained and practiced in their roles and responsibilities. There is a choreographed rhythm to their teamwork and efforts. Our surgeon's job is to synchronize the necessary activities and quickly resolve any conflict or disagreement among her colleagues. In other words, she operates and manages.

Fast-forward two months post-surgery and our cardiologist convenes a meeting with five of her most recent surgical patients. She begins by congratulating them on a successful recovery and informs them she wishes to meet with them individually at regular intervals over the next year to chart their progress. Then she lowers the boom.

All of you are overweight, she says. *Three of you are down right obese. Four of you still smoke. All of you have abysmal diets. All of you drink too much. None of you has followed any sort of exercise routine since high school. These things must change or you may not survive your next cardiac crisis. I intend to monitor your progress toward a more healthy life style at each of our monthly meetings.*

Our cardiologist has decided to lead and she must do so absent any command authority. No longer in the operating suite where she is the boss, she will need to rely upon her persuasive powers, compassionate understanding of the difficult task she has asked her patients to undertake, and her commitment to seeing her leadership role through to its end.[31]

One can just imagine the shocked look on our patient's faces as they contemplate the adaptive work their cardiologist has just asked them to undertake. One can also imagine the inner-doubt some of them feel concerning whether they are up to such a task. Some are probably thinking a second opinion may be in order. Our cardiologist has a lot of leading to do if her surgical survivors are to succeed.[32]

The moment we say yes to the offer of becoming a manager we unwittingly agree to do what our cardiologist did: do our best to both manage and lead and make every effort to realize when to do each. This is a tall order as we quickly discover. Both roles are difficult and stressful, particularly the leadership piece since it so often makes us

31 For a deeper insight into the differences between leading with and without authority, see Ronald A. Heifetz, *The Practice Of Adaptive Leadership: Tools And Techniques For Changing Your Organization And The World* (Boston: Harvard Business Review Press, 2009.

32 This example also appears in a companion book I wrote entitled Effective Organizational Leadership. It is available at Amazon and contains other essential ingredients for leading in today's organizations.

unpopular and generates considerable opposition. Many avoid the leadership role for this reason alone.

To avoid doing the best you can as both manager and leader is an abdication of your responsibilities. That is why the best managers work hard at it and in so doing, help keep their organizations relevant, productive, competitive, and customer focused.

Identity

The Shadow You Cast

Another transition we casually agree to when we say yes to a management job is to assume a new identity. You remember all those conversations where we worker bees complained endlessly about management? Now we are management.

In small organizations, management is perhaps you and the boss. In large organizations, there are hundreds of managers. In either case, to your employees you are still now part of the entire management team, no use pretending otherwise.

Managers who try to distance themselves from the organization's management team look foolish and quickly lose credibility both with their bosses and employees. Think about it, who wants to work for a manager that is not part of the team and thus has little ability to represent the interests of their employees up the line?

Every manager should understand where they fit in their organization's hierarchy. There are commonly three distinct levels to that hierarchy and each level has a critical strategic function. In successful organizations, these levels align in unity of purpose and direction.

At the top of the organization lives **senior management.** Although many managers with longevity and seniority think of themselves as senior managers, the senior management level is a small group. It consists of the CEOs, presidents, or directors, and the heads of the organization's major operating units. Everybody else at this level constitutes staff.

Senior Management's responsibility and critical strategic function is *to set the direction for the organization.* Whether you call it a vision, a strategic goal, or the organization's core objective, the best are expressed in terms that are clear, simple, and thoroughly understandable by everyone in the organization.. More importantly, the goal must be achievable.

This points to the second critical strategic function of Senior Management: ensuring every part of their organization thinks and operates in ways that are consistent with achieving the stated strategic goal. A vision or strategic objective is of little value unless senior management insists on the operating discipline and daily behavior necessary to achieve it.

Take, for example, Apple's vision during the Steve Jobs era: **think different.** It was a vision that Jobs made every effort to ensure drove a passion for innovation that continues to redefine the global world of computing and telecommunication.

At the foundation of an organization lives **line management.** Their strategic function is *to ensure accomplishment of the daily work of the organization.* Line managers can easily recognize themselves because they have no subordinate managers reporting to them. Their direct reports are the organization's daily workforces.

Succeeding as a line manager demands the skill to cope with a broad range of human behavior, especially the ability to motivate effort and initiative, resolve conflict, give directions, and set expectations with clarity. Line managers are option one for answers when employees have questions about organizational goals and objectives, and the meaning of the latest pronouncement from the top. They are essential to the process of directing daily behavior throughout the workforce that furthers and realizes the vision established for their enterprise.

Will line managers provide answers and information consistent with the organizational vision? Will they be able to direct and motivate the workforce in ways that make that vision an operational reality?

Much depends on the success of our third level in the hierarchy: **middle management**. The critical strategic function of managers in the middle is *to translate the vision of senior management into concrete, tangible, usable things.* In organizational terms, I am referring to the programs, policies, daily practices, procedures, resources, and talents needed by line management and the workforce to successfully undertake their work.

Middle managers are intermediaries. They must translate an abstraction called a vision into something concrete, comprehensible, and broadly recognizable as the vision in action. For example, the iPhone, iPad, and PowerBook are Apple's concrete manifestations of innovation.

Middle management is critical to the process of ensuring that important messages communicated up and down an organization are simple, clear, and consistent; everybody hearing about the same thing. When a workforce clearly understands what senior management wants and when every employee can explain the organization's vision to a stranger, middle management is doing its job.

When senior management is frustrated because the workforce does not understand the vision, or when line managers are unhappy with the support and answers they are receiving from above, it is a good bet middle management is failing in its effort to connect the organization's top with those working on the line. No surprise that when organizations choose to thin out their management ranks, the thinning usually occurs in the middle, in hopes of improving top down communication and goal alignment.

There is no such thing as a perfectly aligned organization. Even the most successful organizations have their management dysfunctions and are susceptible to the temptation to stand pat when a changing environment suggests the need for new direction. Nevertheless, to the degree that an organization can achieve a synchronization between its management levels, the chances for business and mission success are dramatically improved.

Wherever a manager fits in this hierarchy, they have their part to play. This is what we call being a corporate team player. Nowhere is this more important or challenging than when you must support a topside decision you disagreed with or make a sacrifice affecting your own unit for the overall corporate good.

We all know many managers who are in it for their own good, jealously guard their turf, and only make corporate sacrifices under duress. This is an abrogation of managerial team responsibility and a sign of a poor manager. When such parochial behavior is commonplace in an organization, whose kidding who when the organization claims it is among the best in its field.

Authority vs. Influence

The Difference Matters

One element of being a manager that lures many to the profession is the idea of having some real authority, of being in control of something, and of having the power to give orders and directions that make things happen. *Power in organizations lies in positions and the people occupying them, not in individuals.*

But what if something a manager wants to accomplish involves goals or objectives requiring the cooperation and involvement of others outside the direct line of their positional authority? What if, given human nature, some of those individuals over whom you have direct authority seem reluctant to do as they're told?

Soon after becoming a manager, most of us come to appreciate the limits of the authority we actually possess. Making decisions and giving orders is one thing, gaining compliance is another. The higher a manager rises in an organization's hierarchy, the more challenging gaining compliance becomes, despite the greater positional authority they possess.

Ultimately, it is not only the authority a manager possesses but also the *influence* they can exert to persuade others to join them in pursuit of specific goals that will determine their success. The best managers are more distinguished for the broad influence they exert over people, objectives and events, than they are for the raw authority they occasionally display.

This reality is succinctly summed up in the late Richard Neustadt's classic definition of US Presidential power as the Chief Executive's ability to persuade, bargain and compromise.³³ According to Neustadt, this search for personal influence "is at the very center of the job of being President" and he notes, "this individual is often described as the most powerful person in the world."³⁴

Unlike the power of authority that resides in a position, the ability to influence cooperation and commitment resides within the character of the manager. One can cultivate a broad network of potentially useful and important colleagues, fill one's Rolodex as they say, but that alone is not enough. What makes others want to work with us are those qualities of personality and character our daily behavior illustrates.

The most influential managers in my experience have all been exemplars of the following character traits.

❖ *The legitimacy of their requests for assistance* -- They do not waste your time with foolish projects or veiled attempts to lure you into doing their work for them. When they ask, the task matters.

33 Richard Neustadt, *Presidential Power* (New York: John Wiley & Sons Inc., 1962), Chapter 3, 33-57.
34 Ibid, viii.

❖ *The Integrity of Their Word* -- You can trust these managers to do what they say. These managers always follow through and honor their commitments.

❖ *Their Commitment to Reciprocity* -- You can count on their reciprocal assistance when you need and ask for it. One of my colleagues suggests a great way you can demonstrate your appreciation for the importance of reciprocity is to remember those who have helped you by thinking of them when you have an extra resource or opportunity. People are always surprised to get something without asking.

❖ *Their Demonstrated Track Record as a Team Player* -- For them it is always about the team and not about the manager and, on this score believe me others can tell.

❖ *Their Willingness to Share the Credit for Success* -- These managers have their egos well in check and their concern for the success and wellbeing of others is evident in their actions. They make certain the limelight shines on everybody.

❖ *Their Open Honesty and Comradeship* -- It is generally fun and rewording to work with these managers. This doesn't mean they are jovial, fun loving, or even funny. They sometimes are tough taskmasters. It is their openness and obvious commitment to the involvement and success of others that makes working with them and being a member of their team desirable.

It is usually helpful and a little humbling to ask one's peers how we stack up when measured against these key traits. The insight gained, however, would tell us a lot about the degree of influence we are likely to exert over the behavior of others. This is important self-insight for somebody who aspires to manage and lead.

The actual power and authority any manager or executive possesses will only take them so far. Without influence that enables their ability to persuade, bargain and compromise, that is about how far they will get.

Your Health

Stress Is a Killer

Recall my story earlier when I was discussing humor, about a colleague who was explaining why she believed work was stressful; it is timed, competitive, and ego involved she told me. I left out the second part of her message. She also asked me to consider how so many of the Type A people who gravitate to management jobs spend their so-called leisure time.

A great many of these Type A personalities engage in so-called leisure activities that share the same three qualities. They become unwitting victims of extensive to-do lists, the paper work they just could not leave at the office, recreational activities where they compete against others or themselves, serious reading just to catch up, and all the work problems they keep turning over and over in their heads. At the end of their leisure time, matters left undone feel like failure. From their body's perspective, there is no difference between leisure and work. It is all stress.

Consider the fact that stress biochemically affects your entire body, especially the musculoskeletal, respiratory, cardiovascular, nervous and endocrine systems. Stress causes the body's muscles to be in a constant state of guardedness. When the body is under stress, the hypothalamus signals the autonomic nervous system and the pituitary gland initiates the process that produces epinephrine and cortisol, often called the stress hormones. These give your body the energy to face danger and stressful work.[35]

Consider that the process never stops until you give your body an unconditional opportunity to fully relax. Many individuals in high stress occupations do this infrequently. Any wonder so many of them suffer from hypertension, Type II Diabetes, chronic pain, sleeplessness, heart issues, stomach and digestive problems, weight gain, ulcers and yes even cancer.

Chronic stress is a physical, emotional and intellectual killer. Being at one's best absolutely demands some balance between work and the rest of our lives. Without some down time, some relaxation, some distance at regular

---

35 See www.apa.orh/helpcenter-body.aspx. An American Psychological Association article entitled *Stress Effects The Body.*

intervals from professional responsibilities, a manager and his workforce are headed for trouble.

It is an unavoidable consequence of our human physiology that when we overwork and overstress ourselves, we compromise our judgment, emotional stability, and the ability to think clearly and rationally about things. Maintaining our sense of perspective on what we do professionally, to say nothing of our health demands we occasionally stop working.

Many managers have challenged me on this point arguing they see it as an unavoidable choice: either accept the workload, hours and stress necessary to be successful or lead a more balanced life at some lower level of responsibility. For me, however, maintaining a balanced life is not an either/or proposition. Rather, it is a fundamental requirement for maintaining sound judgment and clear-headed thinking

Trust me on this point and do it. Start small; leave early one night a week. Start to experience what it is like to feel relaxed so you will be more acutely aware when your body and mind are not. Athletes talk about the necessary recovery time following an event. The smart manager acknowledges and accommodates the regular recovery time demanded by the stress and strain of their responsibilities. The smart manager refuses to wait until their performance starts to slip or worse, they get sick. This is among the most important requirements of self-management.

6.

Unleashing Potential

The signs of outstanding leadership appear primarily among the followers. Are the followers reaching their potential? Are they learning? Serving? Do they achieve the required results? Do they change with grace? Do they manage conflict?

Max Depree author of *Leadership is an art.*

The Magic Formula

You have undoubtedly heard the phrase *there is no magic formula.* When it comes to management, I believe there is. The formula applies to all managers, public or private sector, civilian or military. A formula if you can make it work to its fullest, that is likely to produce extraordinary outcomes.

$$TP + HM = EP$$

Talented people (TP), highly motivated (HM) equals exceptional performance (EP).

Hard to argue against the formula's logic, isn't it? Making it work to our maximum advantage, that is hard. The best managers work at it by paying close attention to the two elements leading to exceptional performance every single day: **talent** and **motivation.**

In his thought provoking book *The Future of Management,*[36] author Gary Hamel addresses the challenge of "reinventing our management systems so they inspire human beings to bring all their capabilities to work every day."[37] Hamel cites a 2005 Towers Perrin survey of 85,000 employees from across the globe that suggests almost 85% of them leave some of themselves behind when they head to their places of employment.

---

[36] Gary Hamel, *The Future of Management* (Boston: Harvard Business School Press, 2007).
[37] Ibid., 58.

According to Hamel, the human capabilities that contribute to competitive success and value-added contributions can be arrayed in a hierarchy with each, scaled something like this:

Passion	35%
Creativity	25%
Initiative	20%
Intelligence	15%
Diligence	5%
Obedience	0%
	100%[38]

All of these capabilities are important to every organization. The bottom three can be acquired through an effective recruitment process. However, obedient, conscientious, well-organized smart people if they are unmotivated, will not provide the initiative, creativity and passion you desire. The imaginative contributions that constantly renew and reinvent what your organization is about, requires skilled management and an entire organization of talented, highly motivated individuals is a wonderful thing to behold.

---

38 Ibid., 59.

Right Mind-Set

How Good Managers Think

Most of us when we first became a manager left a job we had been doing for some time. Perhaps we spent many years of academic study to become a certified specialist and worked tirelessly to establish ourselves as an expert. We enjoyed the esteem in which others held us for our accomplishments.

As a manager, we have accepted a new challenge: stop doing what we were so good at and start getting others to do something. Perhaps this does not sound difficult, but, it is.

The beginning of success as a manager starts in your head. It is grasping completely the nature of the job. The doing part of being a manager is motivating others to do their jobs. The more a manager tries to keep doing the work of those entrusted to them, the poorer a manager they become.

All managers must occasionally get involved in the work they oversee, but how involved and why is the question? Every good manager will tell you it is a perpetual balancing act between getting into some substantive issue and backing off. It comes down to a matter of judgment and motivation. Let us look at a few of the wrong motivations for getting involved:

❖ I am smarter than any of them so why not just do things myself;

❖ I love this stuff so much I just can't let it go;

❖ In the end I'm responsible for this, so I'd better be certain to get it right.

These are all excuses for micromanaging and driving employees crazy. Because these managers will be trying to do two jobs at once, they will underperform at both.

A far more productive mindset involves focusing on two gifts every manager has to give to those entrusted to their management skills: their time and experience. This involves thinking of oneself as an *investor* and *teacher*.

Most managers have been around for a while. They know their organization. They possess many of the same skills and talents of those they supervise. They know how things get done in their organization. They know who matters, whom to talk to, who controls resources, and who can help with this or that problem. This wisdom is invaluable. Investing one's time in teaching others what we know is one of the most important things any manager can do.

When we talk about a manager's role as a mentor and coach, this is what we mean. It is a doing of a different kind for most new managers. Invest and teach well and the backing off becomes much easier. When it works, we discover where the real satisfaction lies in our new profession: the accomplishments of others.

The knowledge that one's skills at a certain specialization will erode and diminish from disuse is ego threatening to many managers. This is especially true when it took years gaining that expertise. However, management done well will produce its own rewards and any regrets will pass.

The mindset of an investor and teacher takes some time to acquire. It is not something most new managers adopt at once. Nevertheless, once a manager begins to focus their attention on growing the talent of others, the backing off challenge becomes less daunting.

Taking Charge

Hit the Ground Learning not Running

Imagine you have not been feeling well for some time. Your symptoms are potentially serious. Persistent headaches, weight loss, digestive problems, low energy, trouble sleeping, etc. You screw up your courage and head to the doctors. The physician you see asks you to describe your symptoms, listens and smiles politely, and then tells you there is lot of this going around. With no diagnostic tests or a physical examination, the doctor writes you a prescription, tells you to take it for a few weeks, and assures you it will do the trick.

How sure are you the doctor has based his judgment on anything more than a hunch? Would you leave the office believing there was little need for a second opinion? Putting yourself in the physician's shoes, would you have prescribed any action without employing your diagnostic tools?

Assume you are taking on a new management assignment. What sort of diagnostic work do you intend before you start changing things around?

Many managers never spend much time thinking about themselves as *organizational diagnosticians.* An organization is an abstract idea, an imagined idea, and a box on an org chart with a name. The people working within it are living, breathing human beings. They are either the right group of people, organized appropriately, managed effectively, and pointed in the right direction, or not. They are happy and motivated, or they are not. They either bring all of themselves to work each day, or are part of Towers Perrin's 85%. A new manager can assume the best but only some diagnostic work will reveal the truth.

Because you are their new boss, your new employees and colleagues will almost certainly have done some checking on your reputation. Even if you are a brand new manager, there will be some pre-existing notion concerning what you will be like and old colleagues are likely to have shared a story or two. Add to this the common belief that like all new managers, you will probably want to change some things, just to place your stamp on your new organization.

While all these pre-conceptions matter to some degree, depending on how strongly they are held, so too does the impressions new manager's personally author during their first weeks on the job. In most instances, these first impressions become a far more accurate indicator of how employees will judge their new boss.

First impressions are a byproduct of behavior. They result from what we do and say. They arise from how we act, speak, carry ourselves, interact with others, and from the choices we make.

While there is an unconscious element to many of our actions, we can manage some of the early impressions we convey by conscious forethought, determined effort, fixed purpose, and consistent attention to reinforcement. Consider, will your new organization initially conclude that you are the dismissive physician anxious to move on to the next patient, or will your behavior signal you intend some serious diagnostic learning before you act?

While I understand the admirable motivation of a new manager to begin doing their job at full tilt, close your eyes and picture a new manager parachuting into a work community with legs churning at high speed. The minute they hit the ground, off they go. Because there are 360 possible degrees in which to run, at least 300 of them are the wrong direction. Consider the damage you might do by quickly imposing solutions for which there are no problems.

How much time should this learning phase take? That is up to you. It is a judgment call. I favor trusting you instinct concerning when you have enough wisdom and data to act.

Talent

Evaluating the Hand You're Dealt

Most managers fantasize about the dream team assignment. We inherit a staff filled with self-starting, bright, multi-talented all-stars who need little management or oversight. All we would need to do is provide a clear sense of direction and get out of the way. Winning performances would follow and others would judge us a gifted and skilled manager. Never happened to me and rarely does to most managers.

Most managers are dealt what I call a mixed blessing. Talent comes in various types and degrees. At times, some of the talent is misplaced, misassigned, or otherwise unsuited to the task. How do you go about assessing the talent you inherit and decide what possibilities they can live into? To answer this question, start by asking yourself this question: *How could I really screw this thing up?*

It may seem an odd question but your answers will lead you to some behavioral approaches representing the antithesis of what you hope to avoid. The following are a few of my suggested behavioral approaches that should help with your talent evaluation and diagnostic work.

1. *Really getting to know those entrusted to your management ability will take time.* An initial conversation with individuals is always a great idea. It is an opportunity to take an early measure of their attitude, self-confidence, and leadership potential. Ask them to share their ideas concerning their own future and about needed improvements in the organization.

2. *Make clear you recognize the good works accomplished before you arrived.* This may include work in progress you ultimately wish to continue. Learn all you can about the past before you deal with the future.

3. *Consistently demonstrate you do not have all the answers by listening attentively to what others think and tell you.* Take notes. Do not be in a hurry to share some grand vision or set of expectations until you have had the opportunity to evaluate what is possible in the near term. You cannot fake this. Demonstrate it by asking questions designed to dig deeper into the respondent's thoughts and perspectives. If you are in a hurry to convey what you want or think about everything, your expressed openness to the thoughts of others will seem fraudulent.

4. *Make clear you have not prejudged people based on your past experience or on what you may have heard.* Most of us want the new boss to judge us with an open mind. This includes those who may have previous experience with the manager in question and those who may have had others bend the new manager's ear about them.

5. *Make clear that you are a behaviorist.* That is, you intend to make personnel decisions based on demonstrated ability without regard for rank, seniority, or self-promotion. Nothing beats what you can empirically verify through your observations when it comes to the work and assignment decisions you must make. Good managers learn to trust their eyes far more than what is written on paper, people's backgrounds, job titles and pay rank, or reputation. It is what people can actually do that matters.

6. *Early on is also a great time for some assignment experimentation.* It is another sign of your open-mindedness and sends a clear signal that you are not likely to typecast and pigeonhole everybody into inflexible roles.

7. *Demonstrate in your actions and decisions that you are seeking a partnership relationship with those entrusted to you.* Consciously sending your new charges this message is beneficial in two ways. First, it signals your willingness and intent to involve those directly affected in making your decisions. It also signals your intent to insist on active employee participation. In time, this will help determine who is on your team and who is not. The best vision and set of performance expectations for any organization are the one everybody has a hand in creating.

Good managers can build toward any vision, but they generally must build. Good managers know they can eventually add to or subtract from their original hand, but it takes time. Signs of a manager's dissatisfaction with their playing hand is a real morale and motivation killer.

The best managers are those for whom talent development becomes a passion and avocation. They are constantly thinking about whom among their charges needs what growth and development opportunities. They are constantly evaluating where each individual is along their potential growth continuum and looking for assignment and task opportunities with the potential to expand their skill repertoire.

Deploying Talent

Goals and Alignment

In 1995, Hollywood released its movie homage – Apollo 13 -- to the US Space Program's most daring space rescue. I have used this example elsewhere, and include it here, because it illustrates so many aspects of good management.[39]

As the crippled spacecraft's crew battled long survival odds 205,000 miles above earth, it suddenly became apparent to ground-based Mission Control that the spacecraft was rapidly running out of breathable air due to near toxic levels of carbon dioxide (CO_2). Mission Control scrambled to help find a solution. The core problem was how to connect two incompatible parts to build an air filter, a contingency they had never remotely considered.

---

39 See Terry Joseph Busch. *Effective Organizational Leadership: The Essential Ingredients* (Available on Amazon), 14-15.

With time measured in minutes, a lead engineer quickly assembled a small team of engineers in a room and deposited several boxes of apparently un-related space items on a table in front of them. "OK people listen up," the lead tells his team. "The people upstairs have handed us this one and we have to come through. We've got to find a way to make this" -- he holds up a square object – "fit into the hole for this" -- he holds up a round object – "using nothing but that" -- he points to the gear on the table, representing the limits of what the spacecraft crew had to work with. "Lets get it organized and build a filter."

This story represents the perfect alignment of an important goal, the right people, the necessary resources, a clear deadline, and a manager exuding total confidence in the team's ability to accomplish the task.

It would be great if a manager could arrange this sort of alignment of talent to task and keep it going indefinitely but, alas, consider the following story of the Kansas City Royals major league baseball team.

In 2014, the Royals suffered a heartbreaking 3-2 loss in game 7 of the World Series at the hands of the San Francisco Giants. Painfully, it happened before their home crowd. To a man, the dejected Royals felt they had been the better team.

During the off-season, Royal players, managers, coaches, and management focused their dedication on one single goal: returning to the post season and winning the

World Series. The team made a few player adjustments in the off-season and, when the 2015 season kicked off the following April, the intensity of their commitment had not changed.

From day one their manager, Ned Yost, seemed to have the magic touch, as he created one productive batting order after another. The first three hitters consistently got on base, the middle of the batting order drove in runs, and the bottom of the order refused to let opposing pitchers off the hook with easy outs.

The team and their fans had a name for it: *keep the line moving.* When a player got hurt or needed some rest his replacement filled in seamlessly. The Royal pitching staff did their job throughout the season and the play-offs. Then it took the Royals only 5 games in the 2015 World Series to claim the championship in a 7-2 victory over the New York Mets.

With that success, what would you predict for the champion Royals in 2016? They finished 81-81, third in their Division and out of the playoffs. What happened to the Royals with pretty much the same team? They proved they were human. Leaving the specifics aside, they proved the alignment challenge is much harder to perpetuate than it may sometimes seem.

Humans are not machines or computers. You cannot program humans to perform consistently. One month they may perform at peak levels and the next they will not. The same alignment that worked so well last year will need adjusting this year and your decisions may prove less magical this time around. Managers must observe and adjust their alignment decisions constantly. Resting on past successes is poor management.

One of the reasons I believe Marcus Buckingham and Curt Coffman's *First Break All The Rules*[40] remains such a staple part of the management literature is the simple, straight forward formula for managerial success their interview data suggests:

❖ Hire for talent not credentials;

❖ Focus on people's strengths and forget what is not there;

❖ Find the right assignments for people, the one's that play to their talents and strengths;

❖ Then define the desired performance outcomes and get out-of-the-way.

This formula is a blueprint for alignment. To accomplish it, you need to know what observed performance tells you an individual can do successfully. My friend and colleague Jack O'Connor calls this knowing an individual's *capabilities* and *capacity*. At what level is an individual capable of performing and how many things can they man-

40 Marcus Buckingham, and Curt Coffman, *First Break All The Rules* (New York: Simon & Schuster, 1999), Chapters 3-6.

age at one time? The value of thinking in these terms lies in several factors.

These two concepts allow you to bypass common indicators like degrees, pay grades and the recommendations of others as predictors of an individual's level of performance. Capabilities and capacity are empirically verifiable through observation. You can either see them or you cannot. This is one reason I have always loved baseball. A player's skills are plainly observable on the field and precisely measurable no matter how they where acquired. This allows the manager to select a young starting pitcher with a 95 mph fastball and low earned run average, over an older veteran whose arm has slowed and earned run average has ballooned.

Relying upon observable capabilities and capacity is also motivational for employees who wish to accelerate their ability to play an important and influential role in your organization. Especially in organizations where seniority or pay grades often determine who gets what plum assignments, shifting the paradigm to one where demonstrated ability outweighs seniority and salary, encourages everyone to show what they can do. Your job as a manager is to ensure that every employee understands the required performance standards and has ample opportunities to demonstrate them.

Focusing on capabilities and capacity allows more flexibility in making assignment decisions. It allows you to assign everyone to those tasks most likely to play to those strengths. As a formula for producing exceptional results, it is hard to beat.

Leapfrogging junior employees over senior colleagues will ruffle a few feathers. However, once you have established that demonstrated ability outweighs anything else in your assignment decisions, you will have established a required performance norm for everyone.

How well does thinking this way really work? Consider the following two examples.

Bruce Bochy is a great manager. His profession is baseball. His San Francisco Giant teams have won three World Series titles, including the 2014 defeat of the Kansas City Royals. Experts considered none of his three championship teams the most talented in baseball that year.

A *Bloomberg BusinessWeek* writer, Diane Brady, interviewed Bochy following his first championship in 2010.[41] His following comments capture some critical insights regarding the alignment challenge in pursuit of grand goals.

❖ *Like any job the more you learn the better manager you become. I was like any young manager when I started out. I was a lot harder on players than I am now. I've learned to be patient.*[42]

---

41 Diane Brady, *Bloomberg BusinessWeek*, November 21, 2010. Bruce Bochy's comments appear on the magazine's final page.
42 Ibid.

❖ *The toughest part of a manager's job is when you have to change the role a player is accustomed to having. Telling a starter that he is now going to be on the bench isn't easy. You're not just dealing with egos; you're dealing with good players who are used to going out there every day.*[43]

❖ *Right now people are saying that I made good decisions, but it always comes down to the players. My job is to put them in a position where they can succeed. They make the decisions look right.*[44]

For the best managers, it is always about people. That is what makes the job so challenging and difficult. Bochy's insight lies in his grasp of the difference between ego and person; between an abstraction and a real human being with their own abilities, capacities, experiences and expectations.

A number or years ago I took a benchmarking trip to Springhill, Tennessee, to observe General Motor's attempt to build a compact car that was not losing money. Saturn was its name.

One of the innovations they decided to try involved tearing up GM's job classification manual and allowing all of their car builders to do any job in their team-based assembly process, provided they could do it safely and up to accepted industry standards.

---

43 Ibid.
44 Ibid.

The result was amazing. I met men and women doing engineering jobs who possessed only a high school degree. They worked side by side with engineering school graduates doing the same job and I believe, their pay was equivalent. How is that for relying on the power of capability and capacity regardless of where, when, or how their learning took place?

Motivation

The Environment Is Everything

The Merriam Webster dictionary defines an environment as follows:

The circumstances, objects or conditions by which one is surrounded.

The aggregate of social and cultural conditions that influence the life of an individual or community.

Unless you work alone, these certainly sound like the components of most workplaces. A workplace has a distinct atmosphere. It has an emotional, almost sensate feel that affects our mood, attitude, enthusiasm, and overall morale. The environment in our workplaces can exert a powerful draw motivating us to abandon our bed in the morning and head to work, or an inhibiting impulse encouraging us to turn over and grab another hour of sleep.

Our working environment matters, because it either encourages commitment, passion, and creativity, or it does not. There is little in between. Those who work there recognize the difference and nobody has as much impact on creating a great working environment than its managers.

Motivational working environments are *trusting* and *nurturing*. They are conducive to teamwork and collaboration. They are environments where people empower themselves, take risks, show initiative, and are willing to take a creative leap knowing their reward will be for the effort not only a successful result. Managers can either encourage or discourage the creation of such environments by the way they behave and I will wager many in the Towers Perrin 85% (see page 123) are victims of management misbehavior.

A fun place to work is a descriptor often attached to highly motivational working environments. Not fun in a giddy or frivolous sense but as places that provide the satisfaction and pleasure derived from hard focused work and successful accomplishment. It is the sort of working environment that makes you occasionally think *isn't it great they pay me to work here.*

Grab your thesaurus and look up synonyms for fun. There you will find concepts like enjoyment, amusement, lightheartedness, and pleasure. Fun represents the behavior and attitude that produces these feelings within us. Wild frivolity, a party atmosphere and a standup comedian are not required. There is nothing inherently antithetical about having some fun at work, provided the bosses set the tone.

The one place I would never have expected to see a fun atmosphere was a factory setting. That was until my Saturn experience. Blaring rock music greeted us as our group toured the factory and smiling faces and waves were common among the car builders busily adhering to the exacting engineering and safety standards for automobiles. Those we spoke with said it was the best working environment they had ever experienced; "a great place to work."

As Carl Jung reminds us: "The creation of something new is not accomplished by the intellect, but by the play instinct arising from inner necessity. The creative mind plays with the object it loves."[45]

No manager, no matter how hard they try, can guarantee a motivational environment to all employees. However, the best managers work very hard to think, act and support those entrusted to them in ways that aim to motivate the best in their daily performances.

Not long ago, my wife and I had dinner at one of our favorite local restaurants. We sat at the bar where my wife enjoys watching the cooking action in the open kitchen area. The Executive Chef and his wife own the restaurant; he manages the back-end while she manages the front.

45   See Brainy Quotes.com, Hashtag Carl Jung.

As my wife delighted in the food preparation, I watched how the floor staff worked cohesively to keep a full restaurant fed and happy. It was clear that the co-owner was in charge but her exercise of authority was so subtle it would have been easy to miss. A glance here, a nod of the head there, a quiet word with a smile as she passed a server, she moved around the restaurant with the rest of the staff pitching in and doing whatever was necessary if something immediate caught her eye. She was clearly in charge of things, yet could easily have been mistaken for just one of the staff.

Hers is what I like to call the quiet exercise of authority. It is a management style designed to motivate and create a working environment where everybody feels part of one team. I asked one of the servers I know whether she liked working for her boss. "Yes", she replied, "she's terrific."

If you wish to assess whether the working environment you oversee meets the test of being a great place to work, put on your diagnostic hat and answer these questions.

1. Is there an easy sense of calm even in the face of heavy workloads, stringent demands for performance, rigid deadlines, and stress?

2. Are mistakes and failures accepted as learning and growth opportunities in a workplace where initiative, creativity, and risk taking are encouraged, thereby making mistakes inevitable?

3. Do employees understand they will be judged primarily by results and not by how they achieve them.

4. Is the predominant philosophy of your organization *hey, we can do this* whatever this is?

5. Is laughter common? Does everybody understand it is the work, not ourselves, we take seriously?

6. Does everybody genuinely care about everybody else's success, not just their own?

7. Does everybody feel respected and believe their accomplishments and contributions are appreciated, big and small?

8. Does everybody fully understand what their organization is about, and can they explain to others how their individual contributions add value to that effort?

How did you do? The point is, the best managers are constantly asking these questions and putting them to their employees for feedback. When they don't like the answers they get, they commit to change.

When it comes to atmosphere make no mistake, the boss sets the tone. Be uptight, your employees will be uptight. Be remote and your employees will sense the cold air and keep their distance. Treat every problem as a crisis and your employees will as well. Lose your focus and sense of direction and others will feel lost along with you. Display uncertainty and doubt on a regular basis and your employees will worry a lot. Conversely, show you really care about the environment you share with your colleagues and they will help you create the environment you want.

One of my favorite management assignments was to an organization known for being overly anxious, up tight, and afraid to make mistakes. When I arrived, morale was low and I had no idea what they expected from an outsider. I sensed uncertainty and a decidedly negative vibe. My first act, motivated by a gut instinct, was to send out a very short all-hands email as I recall something like this: *hi, my name is Terry, this is my first day on the job. I am a little nervous and will need your help.* I am not sure what I expected next but I received quite a few responses of the following type: *relax, we know what we're doing, we will help you.*

Relax, I thought, why not? We spend a great deal of our lives at work, why not have a little relaxation and fun.

Over the following years, I tried to radiate calm, to turn mistakes into learning opportunities, and to encourage having some fun. I wanted the organization to relax while tackling the challenging problems we faced.

Days before I departed for a new job, a customer told me he had noticed a marked difference in our organization over the past few years. "Everybody seems more at ease, positive, enjoying their work. You've made a difference." "Thank you," I replied. "You just made my day."

Think Partnership

Unlocking What You See

What we think we see in others is a perception. Sometimes it is a perception based on observed performance. We call it potential. At other times, it is simply a hunch. Either way, it is enough to stimulate a desire to help encourage what we believe others can do.

The important part is recognizing the other person has a say in the matter. I have had managers tell me they truly believe they know what is best for other human beings. I say, that is an opinion not a fact.

While we may have a definite idea about someone else's potential, we begin to approach reality only when we test our idea against the other person's view and willingness to embrace the effort. Neither of us will know if a certain course of action can achieve its goal until there are results to assess.

Unlocking what we believe we see in others works best as a partnership. Such partnerships should follow three simple rules.

1. Share your perception and views with the other person and really listen to their response. This gives each of you an opportunity to compare notes and search for common ground. Listening for understanding is a powerful sign of respect for those you work with and a great

anchor point for an ongoing and productive interpersonal relationship.

2. If you are asking someone to stretch themselves in new directions, arrive at some agreed upon understandings and expectations. Stretch goals often mean some anxiety for the stretcher. Being real and defining achievable, measurable goals, generally helps produce positive results.

3. If you do not have absolute faith in the ability of someone to achieve a stretch goal, why ask at all. You cannot fake faith in others. It must be genuine. It is something that must reside within.

Think Diversity

Unlocking What You See

Throughout my years as a manager, consultant, and workshop facilitator, I have had the opportunity to compare a large number of groups widely diverse in their composition, with those characterized by homogeneity. What I learned was that choosing a diversity of individuals is a great guiding principle when hiring or selecting a group of people with whom you will be working.

Most humans love sameness. There is comfort and predictability in things that are alike. Sameness unconsciously influences our selection of mates, friends, colleagues, bosses and employees. We are psychologically comfortable being around individuals who behave and think like us.

Diversity or difference introduces uncertainty and unpredictability. Diversity forces us to open our minds to things and ideas that are new, and new ideas carry their reward only after we find our footing outside our comfort zone. I believe this journey beyond comfort is worth it for any manager seeking to unleash potential and manage more effectively.

Diverse groups, by which I mean groups cutting across gender, race, age, cultural background, educational level and work/life experiences, tend to lessen the likelihood of developing an operating mindset characterized by prejudices and stereotypes. Peer pressure is a powerful force and, in this case, the pressure is towards openness and sensitivity.

Diverse groups are less likely to arrive at common groupthink views of the topics they engage. Groups where everybody is alike in gender, race, age, and background experience tend to share a common view. A broad common consensus often isolates anybody offering a different point of view, which in turn authorizes everybody else to ignore what they say. It is very hard for one or two outliers to stand up to the common consensus or sway the views of a larger group.

A multiplicity of views encourages everybody but the most close-minded to open their minds and consider perspectives they might not have generated themselves. There is potentially great wisdom in a collective set of diverse minds. The more diverse a group, the richer and well rounded that wisdom is likely to become.

If you surround yourself with a diverse group of people who will challenge your ideas, present you with their own, argue with you, and force you to support your positions with facts, you will be a better manager. When decisions are required, diverse groups will generally consider a broader range of options and engage in a richer discussion of the pros and cons of each. If you believe, as I do, *there are many roads to Albuquerque so to speak,* why not consider as many reasonable routes as possible. Remember as managers, your job is to get things right, not being the one who was right.

Finally, demonstrating you appreciate the many advantages of diverse thinking teaches and role models that value to those around you. As a designated authority and leader, others watch closely what you do. Talking diversity is fine. Demonstrating you value its contribution to your success is where the real power to influence others lies.

The Power of Psychic Pay

Unlocking What You See

My colleague Jack O'Connor loves to talk about the many ways there are beyond money to reward and motivate as a manager. I call it psychic pay. Our salary pays our bills. Psychic pay satisfies inner desires and needs and opens up many possibilities for managers who are often constrained by tight pay budgets and restricted promotion opportunities.

You must really know and understand those you work with if you are to make the right psychic pay choices. In no special order, here are some of Jack's categories for consideration. They are all within the power of most managers to bestow.

- ❖ *Freedom* — There are those who just love when you give them a task, then leave them alone to figure it out. For those who can handle the free space, freedom and autonomy represent a rich reward.

- ❖ *Responsibility* — Many individuals love being in charge of something. They relish the weight of responsibility on their shoulders and gladly accept it without any significant increase in pay. There are many ways to increase someone's responsibilities without making them a manager.

- ❖ *Skill Mastery* — One path toward upward mobility in most occupations is the mastery of complex skills. Those with a passion for learning and growth will usually thrive when given the opportunity to stretch their skill repertoire.

- ❖ *Visibility* — Exposure is another important ingredient of successful career advancement. No matter how talented we are, eventually all of us require a stage before a live audience to demonstrate what we can do.

❖ *Invisibility* — Some individuals prefer the back stage areas as the arena where they do their best work.

❖ *Routine* — Multi-tasking is not for everyone. Many employees require routine and a defined structure for performing at their best. Finding the right structured environments for these individuals satisfies both their psychic needs and provides a setting in which they are likely to thrive.

❖ *Your Attention* — All employees require the boss's attention from time to time and some need it more than others. I am not suggesting playing favorites, but a manager's attention, strategically employed, is often richly rewarding.

❖ *Travel* — Not all organizations afford many travel opportunities. When available, they are deeply satisfying and exciting for the wanderers among your employees.

❖ *Flex time* — What began as a common organizational practice many years ago has lost most of its original controversial overtones. Arranging flexible working schedules can serve as a powerful motivator for those with outside demands on their time.

❖ *Sense of Impact* — Ask most employees what they
   want at work beyond their paychecks and their answer generally is a version of "I want to make a
   difference." Seeing our work has impact and adds
   an important contribution to an organization's objectives matters a great deal to most of us.

❖ *Being a Mentor* — Helping others succeed is important to many individuals. Offering specific
   mentoring opportunities to individuals with the
   skills, wisdom, and inclination to teach others what
   they know is often a rich psychic reward.

❖ *Being Mentored* - When an employee experiences
   mentoring and coaching from the boss, designed
   to help them achieve mutually agreed upon performance objectives, it communicates the bosses'
   dedication to seeing them succeed. It signals the
   manager's confidence in them. It creates the desire
   in many to work a little harder, go that extra mile,
   and display the initiative and creativity necessary to
   achieve one's goals.

By now, you have the idea behind psychic pay and perhaps have a few categories of your own. None of this works,
however, unless you have invested the time to get to know
and understand what motivates those entrusted to your
management skills. The wrong motivator applied to the
wrong individual generally produces under performance
and unsatisfying results.

Think Teamwork

Unlocking What You See

Managers decide how to align their talent with the work at hand. They can choose to pit individuals against one another in a competitive atmosphere because they believe competition brings out the star players who do the best work. Alternatively, they can align talent in teams because they believe teamwork produces the best overall results for an organization. As to which approach works best, the jury has been in for some time.

Collaborative team efforts generally produce outcomes superior to the performance of a few star players. Many brains and a mixture of skills are superior to what any of us individually know or can do. However, the environment and chemistry must be right for a team to flourish.

Creating an environment that fosters team chemistry is a dream achievement for most managers. Trouble is, human beings are involved. The aggregation of the precise talent, personalities, and the right time and place is an occurrence that defies absolute managerial control. Positive team chemistry requires all team members to set aside their selfish interests for the common good, and no manager can guarantee this happens.

If your goal is a team environment where every individual facilitates the success of everybody else, here are a few ideas. Each of them is well within the capability of good managers and there is considerable evidence that they work.

1. Do not play favorites. Playing favorites is a team chemistry killer. When only certain team members receive special attention signaling their perceived value and importance, the result is resentment, competition, and an every person for themselves attitude.

2. Get to know each team member as individuals. Seeing people as individuals valued for what they personally have to contribute gains their respect. Let them know you expect them to function as a team but you consider teamwork their individual responsibility not yours.

3. Strive to assign team members to a role commensurate with their strengths. Teamwork thrives when you have assembled the right talent and all participants understand and accept their roles. While some roles are larger and more significant than others, every role matters when it comes to outcomes. Finding the right roles for individuals and helping them accept and see the value of those roles, is one thing distinguishing the best managers from their peers.

4. Set team goals combining a stretch with realism. Good teams need goals to motivate them, lest they stagnate and manage only mediocrity. It is a manager's job to help a team define those goals but they must be realistic or frustration will result. If a team's goal will require time and the addition of new team members, your time-frame and benchmarks along the way should reflect that under-standing.

5. Foster a team culture where failure and setbacks become learning opportunities not defeats. Team goal achievement is generally an iterative process demanding effort, creativity, and frequent setbacks along the way. Teams that fail to learn from their failures invariably repeat them. They often evolve a negative team culture where accepting failure becomes the norm. Good managers insist on learning and model it in everything they do.

6. Remove bad apples. Nothing destroys team chemistry and effective teamwork more than a bad apple. Bad apples are those individuals who, for whatever reason, refuse to buy into a team's goals. Bad apples are self-absorbed, motivated only by what they see as their best interest, and are disruptive. Some bad apples are redeemable with the right coaching but, in my experience, most are not. Remove bad apples or team chemistry will suffer.

7. Finally, always have your team's back. When a team succeeds, the manager usually receives their fair share of the credit. The important moments arise when a team fails. The best managers *never*, as the saying goes, *throw their teams under the bus*. Good managers always acknowledge their contribution to any team failure.

Witnessing a terrific team performance is enjoyable no matter the venue. During a business trip to Denver, I was having dinner in Aurora, Colorado. My attention focused

on the three individuals working the bar. The bar was full
of customers and the restaurant was full of diners, most
with a wine, beer, or other drink request. There was plenty
of opportunity for confusion, drink errors, food snafus at
the bar, and unhappy customers. None of that happened
while I was there and I doubt rarely does because those
three individuals were really a team.

They knew their products, balanced friendliness with
concentration, remembered the details, and demonstrated
a commitment to the overall process not individual roles.
I sensed a genuine trust and mutual respect among them.
They represented a living example of the best definition I
have ever seen of a true team: *every team member cares as
much about the success of their teammates as they do about
their own.*

I only had a brief chat with the manager to pass along
some positive feedback and have no idea how she manages
day to day. However, I would be willing to bet she has a
great deal to do with creating a working environment, in
which such teamwork can flourish.

Autonomy and Accountability

Unlocking What You See

Peruse a contemporary book on management and
chances are somewhere within you will find mention of
Google and perhaps Gore and Associates. As companies,

they are modern success stories. Both are innovative and creative, one in the fields of the Internet and algorithms, the other a manufacturing company. Both have similar management philosophies and flat organizational structures.

Dig deeper, and you discover that each company thrives by attempting to maintain a balance between granting freedom and autonomy to their employees in exchange for adherence to rigorous accountability standards.

Consider that surveys often list Google as one of the best places to work in America with what author Gary Hamel calls "its out-sized rewards for out-sized ideas"[46] Google's reputation for cutting-edge innovation and graduate school atmosphere is well deserved.

At Gore and Associates, nobody gets an assignment or works directly for one boss. Rather you select and commit to the assignments you want and teams select their own leaders.

Then remember that Google's and W.L. Gore's working environments are not for the faint-hearted, thin-skinned, or lazy. You have to compete and produce to survive.[47]

How does this autonomy in exchange for accountability balance actually work? You offer adults the freedom to

---

46 Hamel, 102.
47 Ibid., Chapters 5-6.

work in ways suited to their individual skills, strengths, personalities, and preferred work style. In exchange, they agree to be accountable for meeting deadlines, quality standards, deliverables, and customer requirements.

The option of striking this bargain is open to all managers regardless of the type or size of their organization. Managers all across the globe are endeavoring to make the bargain work to get the very best out of their workforce in today's highly competitive world.

Granting autonomy, however, is not the same as authorizing anarchy. Most humans hate anarchy and crave some definable parameters within which to operate. We like to know where the boundaries are, although we are prone to test them occasionally. We want our working environment to have the predictable, familiar, and comprehensible elements necessary for us to function comfortably. Consider as a minimal requirement that everybody should understand management's expectations regarding what they are to do and within what quality and time parameters.

The workforce can then be encouraged to exercise individual initiative and creativity to accomplish goals. The most creative employees will naturally wish to alter and improve upon the overarching structure, but they must have some place from which to begin. Creating that initial place is where to exercise management control.

The challenge is deciding just how much control to exercise and how much to surrender. Over-architect the working environment, and you risk creating restrictions that frustrate initiative and creativity. Under-structure the working environment, and employees often find themselves having to guess precise goals and objectives, thereby leaving outcomes over-exposed to chance.

Management is a performing art and by its very nature, art is a creative process and one filled with trial and error. Most artists tell us they rarely get it right the first time. Gustav Mahler, one of my favorite classical composers, was famous for over-composing his symphonies. He spent years refining and rewriting the scores. Think of your challenge as a constant work in progress; it is a process.

The only way to judge whether you have it about right, is to observe how your employees are doing. Their performance, morale, feedback, and business results should tell you when it is time to adjust some more.

Giving up the managerial control required to grant a considerable degree of autonomy can be scary. But there is compelling evidence that over circumscribed working environments that demand uniformity and insist employees do things a certain way, invariably inhibit creativity, initiative, learning, growth, and quality of output.

On the other side of the bargain, without insisting on accountability for deliverables, simply granting autonomy amounts to authorized play. In Bill Gore's company, for example, all project teams know they ultimately will need to submit their development ideas to the demanding *real–win–worth* corporate test. They must demonstrate their idea solves a real problem, can win a share of the relevant market, and ultimately will provide the company with profits. While senior executives do not expect every development idea to survive this gauntlet, each member of the various project teams understands the consequences of a sustained losing streak.[48]

Defining outcomes with clarity and establishing quality standards is hard in some work environments where output quality is a highly subjective matter of management and customer interpretation. The fact it is difficult, is no excuse for ignoring the potential payoff one gains by effectively striking the bargain.

Undoing Everything

Three Performance Killers[49]

Taking undue credit -- This falsehood is rarely as blatant as claiming a degree not held or Viet Nam service not served. It often happens behind closed-doors when a manager passes off to their boss an employee's idea or accomplishment as their own. In many cases, the innocent victim of this lie remains unaware unless by some chance accident they happen upon the truth.

---

48 Hamel, see Chapter 5.
49   I have written in more detail about these three morale killers in *Habits That Define Poor Managers: A Rogues Gallery*. This book is available at Amazon.

One of a manager's most important responsibilities is *showcasing* an employee's talents, and accomplishments, especially for upper management. Without the manager's willingness to give honest credit where it is due, an employee's path to career success and advancement becomes unfairly harder. Taking behind-the-back credit leaves the employee in the dark, abrogates one of a managers most fundamental responsibilities, and represents a betrayal of the trust and dependency inherent in the superior-employee relationship.

Few managers can hide this deceitful practice for long. Honesty is one personal quality we never wish questioned. Once someone's honesty comes into doubt, the damage is hard to undo.

Bankrupting Your Word -- In Western culture, the phrase *you have my word* has significant symbolic meaning. It is often paired with the concept of honor and it invariably implies a contract between individuals.

I have known my share of managers whose frame of reference for giving their word is politics. For many politicians, changing one's mind for a variety of reasons is perfectly fine and is the nature of the beast. A manager is not a politician.

A manager has far more influence over the lives of those entrusted to them than any politician has over constituents. When a manager promises their employees something, they have given their word. Break these contracts often enough and the value of a manager's word in general becomes suspect. When one's word or promises have little value, trust, loyalty, and a willingness to follow a manager's lead inevitably suffer.

There are times when changing circumstances necessitate revisiting a promise or commitment that no longer is possible or prudent to fulfill. The best managers view these situations as an opportunity for a discussion with an employee aimed at explaining the reasons they believe a different course of action is required. These conversations represent a sign of respect for the employee's ability to fairly consider, if not like, what they hear and make adjustments in their expectations. The best managers never simply renege on a promise.

It has been years, but I still vividly recall the sad after-effects of a broken management promise by one of my employee managers. The manager had given his word on numerous occasions to an employee that a coveted position would be hers as soon as the incumbent moved on. Yet, when the time came to fill the position and I asked the manager for his recommendation, a different person was his choice. Unaware of the backstory, I accepted his recommendation. The aggrieved party, whose anger and sense of betrayal was barely contained, soon confronted me. Within months, the angry employee had departed and the sad tale had spread, damaging the manager's reputation and advancement potential.

Abandoning Ship -- Picture a lively meeting between a manager and his staff. Collectively they have a challenging problem to solve and they are discussing various solutions. In time, two approaches emerge as having the most potential for resolving the problem. However, the manager finds himself in favor of option one, while the staff is strongly inclined toward option two. The discussion continues for a while but it becomes clear the two sides are to remain apart. What next?

The manager, as boss, can simply say, "We are going to do it my way." He is accountable for the outcome and, it is perfectly acceptable for him to make the call. The staff might feel a bit disgruntled but they did have their say.

Suppose, on the other hand, our manager at some point, throws up his hands and says something like: "OK, I'm tired of all this arguing. Enough! Have it your way. We'll go with option two but I know it isn't going to work and just remember, I told you so." This marks the end of the meeting and end of discussion.

What has just happened here? Does our staff of employees feel empowered or abandoned? Does our staff believe their boss will join them in making a full effort to make option two succeed? Alternatively, do they suspect he will silently remain on the sidelines, secretly rooting for the entire effort to fail? In the long run, for the sake of group cohesiveness, would it have been better for the boss to have insisted on option one, rather than take the course he did?

At its best, a manager/employee relationship resembles a partnership. Each side has a role to play. Once there is a decision, managers expect full effort from employees to achieve a successful outcome. In exchange, employees expect full commitment from their manager to help achieve success and a willingness to share responsibility for any failures that result. The popular phrase is *having their backs*.

Few employees will put up with, let alone work at full capacity for, an abandoning manager. Even fewer competent senior executives will view such behavior by a junior manager as qualifying them for senior management responsibility.

7.

Being Understood

*The single biggest problem in communication is
the illusion that it has taken place.*

George Bernard Shaw

Two monologues do not make a dialog.

American Architect Jeff Daly

It is Hard

Really, Really Hard

Earlier I noted almost everything a manager does involves human beings. Here I extend that statement to say almost everything a manager does involving human beings, requires some form of communication: face to face, before a group, over the phone, or in some written form.

I suspect every manager, when communicating hopes to achieve understanding. Unfortunately, the human communication process makes the achievement of this challenging goal extremely difficult.

The following is a simplified look at the process. It begins with a thought biochemically produced in our emotional mid-brain. The thought, as we become consciously aware of it, represents something we wish to convey to another.

The next step is a translation activity. We must choose from our extensive vocabulary the exact words we believe represent the thought we wish to communicate. How much this word selection process is subject to our willful control as opposed to additional biochemical activity is a mystery modern neuroscience is still pursuing.

Once we select our words, we communicate them in some format to the desired audience and here is where the process gets interesting. Let us say a single individual is the target of our message. While we are concentrating on the words of our message, the recipient is receiving three messages simultaneously:

❖ The Words;

❖ Our Tone of Voice;

❖ Our Non-Verbal Behavior.

The perceived messages conveyed by our tone of voice and body language represent the recipient's interpretation of our feelings and attitudes. Although we may be totally oblivious to them, they register almost immediately. To achieve full understanding, our recipient must re-translate our words into the meaning they attach to them. Our perceived feelings and attitudes communicated non-verbally will affect that word interpretation especially if inconsistent.

Psychologist Albert Mehrabian is widely known for his experimental findings suggesting that only about 7% of a communication received is contained in our words. Mehrabian's studies found roughly 38% of the message attributable to our tone of voice and 55% to our body language.[50]

Mehrabian's findings have been controversial, challenged, oversimplified, and overused. However, subsequent attempts to replicate his experiment have failed in

---

50 See rightattitudes.com/albertmehrabian 2008.

any statistically significant way to undermine the relative distribution of the weight and impact carried by these three elements.

The important point is this: when our words disagree with our tone of voice and body language, others are likely to believe the message our non-verbals convey.

You might ask what happens with phone conversations without body language or with email, texts, or tweets without both a tone of voice and a visual? Communication experts have studied both situations and the results are dismaying. With only words to go on, we tend to intuit a tone of voice and non-verbal message. That's right, we make it up.

When I was discussing this point in one of my workshops, a manager blurted out "now I understand why he thought I was angry." I asked him to explain. He told the class he had sent a one-sentence email to a colleague and got a phone response asking him why he was so mad.

It is not difficult to see how misunderstandings can and do occur. All good managers comprehend this difficulty and few are confident full understanding results from their communications. Consider the following Harvard Business Review article by Chip and Dan Heath, professors of Communication at Stanford University, as additional evidence justifying their skepticism.

In 1990, a Stanford University graduate student in psychology named Elizabeth Newton illustrated the curse of knowledge by studying a simple game in which she assigned people to one of two roles: tapper or listener. Each tapper was asked to pick a well-known song, such as Happy Birthday, and tap out the rhythm on a table. The listener's job was to guess the song. Over the course of Newton's experiment, 120 songs were tapped out. Listeners guessed only three of the songs correctly: a success ratio of 2.5%. However, before they guessed, Newton asked the tappers to predict the probability that listeners would guess correctly. They predicted 50%. The tappers got their message across one time in 40, but they thought they would get it across one time in two.[51]

The tapper's overconfidence was based on them knowing exactly what they were trying to communicate. They could hear the tune in their heads. Most of the listeners heard only a confusing tapping noise and had little idea what the tune might be.

The best managers, no matter how glib and articulate, usually have a raft of stories to tell about what they learned from their communication snafus. Thus, when a communication is important, they rehearse in advance and strive for precision in the language they choose. They follow-up with repeated efforts to convey the essence of the same message in various forms. They develop the ability to ask questions designed to ascertain the message others believe they have received. This allows them to make subtle shifts in emphasis to clarify any confusion.

---

51 Chip and Dan Heath, *The Curse Of Knowledge,* Harvard Business Review, December 2006

If this sounds like hard work, it is. Managers exert their influence on most matters via their written and oral exchanges. When it really matters, the effort required to insure clarity and a common understanding is well worth it.

In the sections to follow, I offer a few thoughts on some of the things I learned and that worked for me. They are far from a comprehensive exploration of the communications topic but should stimulate some ideas of your own.

Speak In Plain Language

The One without the Jargon

If you work for an organization of reasonable size, you understand when I say that management often speaks in gobble-de-gook. This language turns management initiatives into alphabetical soup like ADIM -- Advanced Data Information Management -- or NGAD -- Next Generation Automotive Development -- and then begins to pronounce them as if they were actual words.

Why does this happen? In part, because strategic initiatives like the fictitious ones I created above are complex and multifaceted. It just seems simpler to try to capture a sense of the entire thing in an acronym and assume that everybody will end up with the same general sense of its meaning.

Also at work is what you might call the *copycat effect.* Most organizations seem to do it, so we will as well. It becomes a matter of how managers communicate with each other by habit.

Consider this copycat effect at work in the common jargon that often populates management speak where simpler words and phrases would suffice. For example, the use of:

❖ Synergy rather than cooperation;

❖ Conflate rather than combine, blend, or bring together;

❖ Alignment rather than agreement;

❖ CONOPS rather than this is what this thing is for and how you should use it;

❖ Instantiate rather than incorporate, express, or provide a specific example;

❖ Incentivize rather than encourage;

❖ Touch base rather than meet or talk;

❖ Cross-fertilize rather than teach;

❖ Interoperability rather than share and use information;

❖ Horizontal integration rather than work together;

❖ Off-line rather than not here;

❖ Bandwidth rather than intelligence;

❖ Analytics rather than facts or data;

❖ Cascade rather than communicate to others; or

❖ Low hanging fruit rather than the easy stuff.

Soon after I entered the professional world, an editor informed me my written products demonstrated a high FOG index. Hoping it was an acronym with some positive connotation, I asked her to explain. She told me it indicated an excessive use of words that many average folks would not understand; indeed, it meant fog. In hindsight, her feedback was a blessing that started me on a quest for simplicity and clarity in my oral and written communication.

The people who most need to understand the true meaning of management-speak are the workforce. Acronyms and jargon are not the way they converse. In many cases, communications filled with jargon and fancy words go right past them. In plain language, they often do not know what the hell management is talking about.

New initiatives, ideas, processes, and systems generated by management generally have a positive purpose. They aim to make work easier, more efficient, more productive, and beneficial for the organization. But what the workforce wants to know about something new is how it will affect them personally, whether it will change their job, and how and whether they will have any say in the matter.

These communications require plain language so understanding and give and take dialog can occur. If a workforce needs to understand how they are part of something new, they need to understand it in their terms and feel management is listening to them in their language when it comes to constructive feedback.

As an illustration of why plain language beats jargon, consider the value of plain language in creating a powerful mission or vision statement for your organization. I have sat through many a painful meeting arguing over words, embellishing adjectives, ego-boosting descriptions and ended up with a long complex mission statement the workforce simply ignored.

A mission statement should simply state what an organization is about.

❖ **"Make People Happy"** -- The Walt Disney mission summed up in three words.

❖ **"Just Win Baby"** -- The mission of the Oakland Raiders when owned by Al Davis. Also three words.

❖ **"Organize the world's information and make it universally accessible and useful."**[52] OK, eleven words but its simplicity and authenticity communicates clearly to all Googlers.

A vision statement should simply and clearly communicate a sense of how an organization wishes to go about its mission.

❖ **"Think Different"** -- This was Steve Jobs vision of the how at Apple. Many wanted to change different to differently but Steve would have none of it. Differently places the emphasis on how one is thinking. Different emphasizes about what one is thinking. Steve's vision was new things.

❖ Google sums up its vision in support of their mission in three words: **mission, transparency and voice.** The how at Google is placing mission first, ensuring that everybody is fully informed about everything (no secrets), and guaranteeing everyone has an opportunity to express their views regarding the work they do every day.[53]

You get the picture. If you wish your workforce to understand you, speak in their language and keep it simple.

---

52   Laszlo Bock, *Work Rules: Insights from Inside Google* (New York: Hachette Book Group, 2015), 33.

53   Ibid., Chapter two *Culture Eats Strategy for Breakfast,* 29-53.

Code Words and Phrases

Beware Their Hidden Meanings

A favorite saying at Google is *culture eats strategy for breakfast.*[54] Culture defines a working environment. A positive environment stimulates creativity and productivity. A negative environment frustrates both and no strategic vision, regardless of its brilliance, can overcome that. Listen to the words that permeate a working environment and they speak volumes about a culture and what it is like to work there.

Language is powerful. Consciously or unconsciously, words create and convey evocative, emotional images for both user and receiver.

Most organizations and their managers develop their own particular language to describe their business, products, employees, daily work practices, culture, competition, and customers. This language consists of words, phrases, and concepts conveying descriptions and images that become so common in daily parlance we hardly recognize them as habitual means of expression. New employees pick up these words and turns of phrase almost unconsciously and rarely stop to dwell on the actual images and messages they convey.

Ask yourself, for example, is it common in your organization to hear the pronouns I, me, my, and mine, rather

---

54 Ibid., 29.

than us, we and our. These words reveal a great deal about culture. I, me, my, and mine convey a focus on individuals, possessiveness, and who owns what; my people, my administrative assistant, my employees, my unit, my resources. The implication is generally *hands off*. Us, we and our, conveys a collective focus and a sense of sharing responsibility, people, and things. If your organization preaches and is serious about teamwork, corporate thinking, and shared responsibility which pronouns should you hear most often?

Similarly, pay close attention to the words and phrases used to describe your competitors, customers, internal units, management, employees, and especially poor performers. Are these descriptions and the images they conjure up reasonable, respectful, logical and accurate? Or are they derogatory, demeaning, and disrespectful?

In one of my workshops, a participant described the reassignment of a poor performer he nicknamed Joe Schmuckatelie as passing the trash. While I did not believe he truly viewed a fellow human being as a schmuck or trash, what does this phrase, if commonly used, say about his organization's culture?

Since most organizations make a clear distinction between the professionals who work in core business or mission areas and those employees who work in the enabling support infrastructure, pay attention to how one group describes the other. Do these descriptions convey a sense of recognition that everybody contributes to business success, or do they convey a sense of class distinction and unequal importance and value? Talk especially to the support professionals, they have keen ears and long memories.

When an organization routinely refers to its employees as resources, they unconsciously relegate them to the same category as computers, tables and chairs. When managers use the phrase *opening our kimonos* to indicate their desire to share or not share information, watch the women in the room cringe because this is probably only one of the frequently used sexist phrases. When managers describe a variety of behaviors as that *touchy feely stuff*, they are pejoratively dismissing things like feelings and human needs as emotion-laden behaviors best left to others, preferably women. How unfortunate, since being in touch on an emotional level is a vital part of every good manager's repertoire.

I repeat, language is powerful and can work either in support of management goals or to their detriment. Eliminate negative, inappropriate, disrespectful, and dismissive modes of expression. Call others out when you hear them. Censor yourself to set the right example. It takes time to evolve a new culture in any organization so start now.

Don't Bury the Lead

What is the Point?

The late author Nora Ephron often recounted the story of her first day in Charles Simms' journalism class at Beverly Hills High School.

My *high school journalism teacher, whose name is Charles O. Simms, is teaching us to write a lead, the first sentence or paragraph of a newspaper story. He writes the words "Who What Where When Why and How" on the blackboard. Then he dictates a set of facts to us that goes something like this: "Kenneth L. Peters, the principal of Beverly Hills High School, announced today that the faculty of the high school will travel to Sacramento on Thursday for a colloquium in new teaching methods. Speaking there will be anthropologist Margaret Mead and Robert Maynard Hutchins, the president of the University of Chicago." We all sit at our typewriters and write a lead, most of us inverting the set of facts so that they read something like this, "Anthropologist Margaret Mead and University of Chicago President Robert Maynard Hutchins will address the faculty Thursday in Sacramento at a colloquium on new teaching methods, the principal of the high school Kenneth L. Peters announced today." We turn in our leads. We're very proud. Mr. Simms looks at what we've done and then tosses everything into the garbage. He says: "The lead to the story is 'There will be no school Thursday.'"*[55]

---

55 See simplicityrules.com, *Don't Bury the Lead.*

This is one terrific story. It is about the point, and your audience and your message determine the point.

The lead is the primary message you wish to convey and, since your aim is understanding and recall, your primary message is where you should begin. Earlier I noted how important the first few sentences are of any conversation. They set the tone for all that will follow and they contain the information your listener will most likely remember.

When your communication is important, prepare the opening carefully. The best professional athletes study film before events to prepare for the opponent they will face. I once asked a neurosurgeon what he did before a major surgery. He told me he studied every test result and went over and over every visual image because he wanted no surprises once he got inside somebody's head.

The best managers think out the lead before hand. They practice the words. They sometimes try them out on others to gain their feedback. They are determined never to bury the real point of a communication if they can help it.

Our Attention Span

It's Limited

As important as the lead message is to any critical communication, so is awareness of the limits of the human attention span. Listening or paying attention for an extended time is a challenge for most human beings.

How long most of us will listen to anything, pay attention to anything, or stick with something we are reading, primarily depends on two things: our interest in the subject and the time it takes the speaker or author to get to the point. I have asked many people to estimate how long it takes them before their mind starts to wander if confronted with a form of communication that does not grab their attention almost at once. The answers have varied but three minutes seems about the outer limits.

Humans have a natural economy of attention. Grabbing that attention, holding it, and communicating an understandable message requires some strategic thought. In their fascinating book *Made to Stick* authors Chip and Dan Heath explore what it is that makes certain ideas stick with us while others fade like mist. Although their book sells under the advertising label, many of their insights are spot on for communication in general.

Think about the following Heath brother's insights when confronting the short attention span likely to greet almost any of your important management communications. Ideas that stick, argue the Heaths, follow a basic formula. They are:

- ❖ **Concrete** — these are ideas that express or conjure up images of *tangible, specific realities*. We can see, touch, hear and experience them directly. Abstract ideas only make it harder for us to comprehend their meaning.

- ❖ **Simple** -- they express *the core of the idea* and are compact and short in expresion.

- ❖ **Credible** — that is, *we as the source of the idea possess a credibility that makes us believable*. We have what the Heath's call testable credentials to back up the validity of what we say.

- ❖ **Emotional** — these are *ideas that have the power to make others care about them*. Emotional ideas draw upon the emotions and self-interest of others. Emotional ideas make clear why they matter to the listener or reader.

If you can couple these four qualities with brevity and succinctness of expression, you are well on your way to counteracting a short attention span. This is why high quality newspapers take such pains to capture the essence of a story in their headlines. Peruse a few of the leading news periodicals and note the brief essence-summaries often preceding the more detailed articles covered later. They know many readers will go no further than the summaries.

The best communicators never forget they have a limited span of time to capture the listener or reader's attention.

Repeat What's Important

Often

Say you have communicated a message to someone, in some form. It is an important message and the last thing you want is miscommunication and misunderstanding. You grasp the consequences if misunderstanding occurs. How confident are you that your communication job is complete upon first broadcast?

We can do little to alter the mental and physiological elements of the communication process. There are, however, two elements of the process we can control: intended message and its reinforcement.

To assume even one individual, let alone a group or crowd, clearly understands a message precisely as intended is a fool's game. I recall watching over three hundred individuals departing an auditorium after I had given a presentation and saying to a colleague "well there goes at least two hundred and fifty different interpretations of what I just said.

When the communication matters, follow up is critical. You may change the words a bit but the message and key ideas should always emerge. Because many of us tend to test whether something is real repetition of important communications helps convince resisters you mean what you say. While being known as somebody who constantly repeats themselves is often an insult, for managers seeking understanding, repetition is sometimes essential.

Dialogue Don't Monologue

Can we talk?

When we hear the term presentation, we tend to think of something prepared, something formal, something thought out and through ahead of time. A presentation is generally lengthy not a spontaneous response. The term presentation also suggests a monologue where a person or tag-team delivers prepared remarks on some specific subject, often accompanied by graphics.

There is nothing wrong with a presentation in the right context, on appropriate subjects and at reasonable length. Presentations are essential to modern-day business and government work.

However, presentations represent a one-way form of communication where audiences are expected to listen, take notes, stay awake and focused, stop checking emails and messages on their smart phones, and remember some of the important points. Even when a question and answer segment is part of a presentation, the answers are usually another form of monologue.

A dialog, on the other hand, is where we stand the greatest chance of learning something important. An effective dialog is a form of conversation in which individuals engage a topic and exchange information, facts, and points of view. An effective dialog is one where all parties listen to one another with mutual respect for different perspectives and the reasons they exist. Reaching total agreement is not the point. Learning something and broadening one's own perspective is.

Are you wondering if your communications are clear and understood? A dialog will help you find out. Dialog allows you to ask questions, provide clarifications, and seek important feedback, allowing for adjustments to support your initiatives and management decisions.

More importantly, honest dialog creates a rapport that reinforces the message that we are all in this together. It signals you understand there are many sides to things and that the folks who will be affected by your management decisions have a right to weigh in on matters that will impact their work lives.

Think about how you communicate with others. If you are primarily a broadcaster whose main interest is conveying your thoughts and opinions, you are chiefly a presenter. Even those most skilled at delivering a presentation are usually not very effective learners when addressing an audience.

By contrast, the most effective managers are invariably also skilled conversationalists. They are adept at the art of dialog. They prefer asking far more questions than the number of opinions they express. They weigh carefully the value of the answers their questions elicit and are willing to adjust their own positions when presented with a better idea or information that warrants it.

Many heads are usually smarter than one. A presentation represents our own thinking. A conversation generates collective thought and often a better, well-rounded perspective on the topic at hand.

Communicating Decisions

What Exactly Did You Decide?

A common complaint I hear from employees is they often do not understand the decisions their managers have made. Yes, sometimes they don't wish to understand. Sometimes they listen selectively. Sometimes they search a communication for just those parts they like and stay focused on that. Sometimes they do understand but enjoy pretending they do not. However, sometimes the real problem is simply a poor management job at communicating the decision.

While I do not believe most managers are intent on deliberately keeping their workforce in the dark, I do believe there is often a bit of laziness involved when it comes to thinking through an explanation of the what and why a decision was made. Some decisions such as everybody can take Friday off require little or no explanation. As a rule, however, managers should spend time crafting an effective communication message, proportional to the importance of the decision itself.

Let me wrap up this section on being understood by suggesting a simple formula for communicating your decisions that conforms to the basic principles of plain language, brevity, leading with the lead, and respect for the receivers attention span.

1. **Keep the message short.** Nothing distracts more than a plethora of words. If you write the message, I am a big fan of the one-pager. You can always say more about an important decision but be brief in communicating the decision's essence.

2. State the decision. Ask yourself the simple question -- what exactly did I or we decide -- then write it down and make certain you are satisfied with the answer. Limit yourself to one sentence.

3. Explain the reasoning behind the decision. The goal here is not to sell the decision. Rather the goal is to explain what the decision means to accomplish. Ask yourself --what do I or we hope to achieve with this decision -- then express the answer in no more than two sentences. This explanation says you thought about the matter with some care and had a plausible rationale for the decision.

4. Stipulate how you intend to measure the decision's effectiveness. Not only is this often not part of a decision's communication to a workforce, worse, it is often not a serious part of the decision making process itself. Think of this as a variant of the saying *if you don't know where you are going, how will you know when you get there?*

Letting a workforce know that you intend to measure results, and sharing the measures you intend to use, is a powerful message that enhances your managerial credibility. It indicates you understand there is no such thing as a decision until you have implemented it and observed the results.

Communicating your measures for success is especially important to those who may disagree with your decision, letting them know there will be a re-evaluation of the results. It gives you a method of testing the judgment call and act of faith your decision represents.

5. Finally, indicate exactly when you will undertake a re-evaluation of the decision's impact. Putting an exact time frame on the re-evaluation process lends credibility to the promise it contains and necessitates some form of tracking process to fulfill the promise. Do not fail to put this tracking process in place.

To promise things you do not deliver is poor management. Even the most effective communication messages regarding a decision will not serve you well if they end up being false or unfulfilled.

8.

Students of Their Game

Learn as if you were to live forever.

Mahatma Gandhi

Learning is not attained by chance.
It must be sought for with ardor and diligence.

Abigail Adams

The final thing I believe the best managers intuitively grasp is the importance of being a student of their game. Playing a game well is a matter of talent. Managing the game well requires an in-depth understanding of all its complex dynamics. Gaining that understanding is a learned achievement acquired over time.

At 46, Sarah Blakely is a self-made billionaire. She is the founder and sole owner of a woman's undergarment company called *Spanx*. Many have referred to her story as the "American Dream."

Sarah had never taken a course in business and had no background experience in fashion, retail, manufacturing, or advertising when she decided to create her product. However, her success would be no accident. She transformed $5,000 in personal savings into a $500 million dollar-a-year company by never taking "no" for an answer and teaching herself everything she would need to know.

As she told Fareed Zakaria in a CNN interview in August 2013:

Well, my inspiration for Spanx was actually my own butt. So I don't know if this has ever happened to you, Fareed, but I could not figure out what to wear under my white pants. And like so many consumers out there, we have these clothes that we can't figure out what to wear under them. And so the panties show the panty line and the shapers were too thick and bulky. So by cutting the feet out of my control top pantyhose, I realized, you know what, this hosiery material that's second to skin would make really good undergarments and shapers meant to be hid-

den under the clothes that smooth us out and get rid of the panty line. And Spanx sort of filled this niche between two options of undergarments, that neither one were quite right for women, and revolutionized the way that we got to wear our clothes. "[56]

Armed only with the experience of hearing "no" often during her seven years of selling fax machines door to door, Sarah used the Internet to find potential hosiery mills to manufacture her idea.[57] She wrote her own patent because most attorneys she approached laughed at her idea.[58] Numerous potential manufacturers turned her down until one in Charlotte, NC, agreed to undertake the task only because his two daughters told him Spanx was a terrific idea.[59] Sarah taught herself the ins and outs of appropriate sizing and she self-marketed her product to the likes of Saks Fifth Avenue and Neiman Marcus, succeeding with the latter only after convincing the buyer she interviewed to try on a pair.[60]

Sarah Blakely has revolutionized the world of women's undergarments through the power of determination and learning. Spanx are available in over 50 countries worldwide. Sarah owns 100% of her company, has no outside investors, and spends no money on advertising. Why bother. After an Oprah Winfrey endorsement, Spanx sold

56 See YouTube, Sarah Blakely's interview with Fareed Zakaria, August 24, 2013, Global Public Square on CNN.
57 See You Tube., Sarah Blakely's Keynote Address 2012, The Edge Connection.
58 Ibid.
59 Ibid.
60 See You Tube, Fareed Zakaria Interview.

20,000 pairs.[61]   Sarah succeeded by becoming a student of the product development process.

Bill Gates, legendary founder of Microsoft and now a global philanthropist, was born to good fortune. As author Malcolm Gladwell explains, his wealthy Seattle, Washington, parents pulled him out of public school in the seventh grade and enrolled him at Lakeside, a private school populated by the children of Seattle's elite. Lakeside had the funds to found a computer club, a rare thing at most colleges at the time and Bill found a new home.[62]

From that time on, writes Gladwell, Bill lived in the computer room. When Lakeside closed its club, Bill and his friends started gathering at the University of Washington, which had free computer time between 3:00 and 6:00 in the morning. Soon he discovered a company called Information Sciences, Inc., which offered more free computer time in exchange for working on some software development.[63]

By the time Bill Gates dropped out of Harvard to start his own software business that became today's Microsoft, he "had been programing practically non-stop for seven consecutive years."[64] Through practice and indefatigable energy Bill Gates establish his bona fids as a student of the programing art.

---

61 Ibid.
62 Gladwell, Outliers, op.cit., 51-52
63 Ibid.
64 Ibid. 54-55.

J.K. Rowling's story is well known. A single unemployed mother on public assistance, her struggle to become a published author began in the back room of an Edinburgh café overlooking Edinburgh Castle. She had no formal training as a writer or journalist and knew almost nothing about the publishing business. She would have to learn.

Seven magical Harry Potter books later, a major motion picture released for each and millions of dollars richer, we can say Ms. Rowling has learned well. Bear in mind, a dozen publishers rejected her first manuscript, she knew nothing of marketing, nor anything about the franchising and movie rights agreements she would eventually confront. She had a great deal to learn to become one of the most celebrated authors of her time.

Perhaps none of the above stories carries quite the fascination of the Wright Brothers tale. Born in Dayton, Ohio, in the late 1800s to an itinerant clergyman and his wife who died early of Tuberculosis, the Wright brothers were described as "self-contained, ever industrious and virtually inseparable."[65]

Orville started his own printing shop before finishing high school in 1889, and the two brothers started a small bicycle business in 1893.[66] The closest thing to flight was Wilber's fascination with bird watching.

---

65   David McCullough, The Wright Brothers (New York: Simon and Schuster, 2009), 6.

66   Ibid., 18-22.

David McCullough, the Wright brothers biographer, notes it was a time of invention in America, and Dayton had an atmosphere where inventing and making things was part of the culture. The bothers found interest in flight and inspiration in the writings and experiments of men like Louis Pierre Mouillard, a French farmer and student of flight, Octave Chanute a French born American Civil Engineer, and Otto Lilienthal, a German glider enthusiast who died in his own experiment.[67] Gradually, as McCullough describes it, the dream of manned flight took hold.

They would design and build their own experimental glider-kite drawing on much they had read, much they had observed about birds in flight, and importantly from considerable time thinking. They had made themselves familiar with the language of aeronautics, and the terms used in explaining the numerous factors in attaining equilibrium otherwise known as balance in flight.[68]

In the years to follow, they would face numerous setbacks and failures. Accidents occurred, some serious, but they studied them for clues and moved forward. Many thought they were crazy, but again, as McCullough writes:

In no way did any of this discourage or deter Wilber and Orville Wright, any more than the fact that they had no college education, no formal technical training, no experience working with anyone other than themselves, no friends in high places,

---

67   Ibid., 31-37
68   Ibid.

no financial backers, no government subsidies and little money of their own. Nor did the entirely real possibility that at some point, like Otto Lilienthal, they could be killed.[69]

When you stop to think about what the Wright brothers needed to learn to achieve their historical success, it is almost staggering. They had little choice but to engross themselves in every aspect of flight design starting from scratch.

At this point, you may wish to take issue with my choice of subjects, pointing out they all became famous and successful people. They are certainly not exemplars of the average Jane and Joe most of us consider ourselves.

However, we most likely would not know much about any of them had they not dedicated themselves to the learning curve challenges each faced. In my immediate family, I have a son who became a successful wine professional by learning everything from harvesting grapes to the fine art of tasting, a daughter who has succeeded at several occupations each with steep learning curves, and a wife who decided to become a Master Gardner through classes, reading, and substantial hands on experimentation.

If you look into your own experiences, I am certain you will find examples of ordinary people who developed a passion for learning about some area of intense interest, stayed with it, and became students of one occupation or another.

---

69   Ibid., 35.

This is how the best managers get to be as good as they are. There are no shortcuts. They work at it every day. Recall, I began this book discussing what we learn about the value of hard work and what it teaches us in the books by George Will, Malcolm Gladwell, Carol Dweck and Geoffrey Colvin.

The best managers are life long learners. They study their experiences, their successes and failures, for the valuable lessons they teach. They read, discuss their management challenges with their colleagues, and are never satisfied they know it all. If you want to master the art of any profession, you must become its devoted pupil.

9.

Apply Your Learning

The preceding sections of this book aim to sharpen your skills and insights into the dynamics of management. The following 32 scenarios offer an opportunity to put what you've learned to work. Spend some time considering how you would handle each of the following situations. Discuss them with colleagues. These situations occur daily in organizations across the globe.

There are no correct answers to any of these scenarios. The point is how would you handle them? Be aware, each scenario is more complicated than may appear on the surface. Some have multiple layers and challenges you will need to confront to reach a satisfactory outcome. How do you think the best managers cope with these challenges?

1. You are finding your first management assignment more difficult than you imagined. You miss the acclaim and recognition you received as a talented specialist, recognized widely as a true expert in your field. You are feeling lost at sea as you endeavor to come to grips with the management profession, and find some job satisfaction. What do you do?

2. Your boss criticizes you for the quality of a product or service produced by one of your teams. The problem is you thought it was just fine when you reviewed it. How do you respond and what actions do you think you should take?

3. You work for a boss who is often critical of the things you do. She always seems to find a hidden flaw. She characterize her feedback as constructive input but you often experience it as a sign she has little faith you are up to your job. How do you intend to manage the troubling emotions associated with this situation?

4. Since you took your current job, you have had the feeling your boss does not personally like you. The two of you do not seem to click. While there is little specific you can put your finger on, he does seem to have more confidence in, and a better relationship with, the rest of your manager colleagues. Is this a problem? If so, why? If not, why not?

5. This individual has long been one of your organization's most dependable performers. Recently her productivity has fallen off and so has the quality of her output. You are concerned but see no obvious reasons for the decline in performance. Is there a problem here? If so, what is it and what will you do and why?

6. You and a colleague competed for your current management assignment. You won and the colleague now works for you. The colleague's morale and effort have declined. You are concerned your colleague may now be disinclined to follow your lead. What, if anything, should you do?

Imagine a similar scenario where you have been appointed head of the organization that currently employs you. Many of your new employees are friends. How do you plan to manage this situation?

7. You have recently given a young employee their first performance review. It is, in your judgment, a solid review with many positives, and a few key development challenges. During your review session the employee's reaction seemed positive and accepting. Two days after presenting the evaluation, you receive a phone call from the employee's parent or significant other suggesting your failure as a manager to recognize the individual's talents and potential. What steps do you need to take?

8. In a casual conversation, a senior manager makes several negative comments about one of your employee's skills and potential. You believe these comments are unfair and ill informed. Caught off guard and absent a ready response, you let it pass. Nevertheless, you are concerned these impressions will endure and perhaps spread to your employee's detriment. What, if anything, should you do?

9. A relatively new employee tells you they do not intend to stay with your organization for very long. They tell you they see your organization as a great place to learn new, portable skills and take advantage of training opportunities. Currently their work output, creativity, and initiative are among the best in your organization. How do you feel about this and how do you respond to them?

10. One of your employees excels at seeing the negative in just about everything. Their negativity is a common component of your staff meetings and the underlying message in any email they send up the chain of command. Once this individual latches onto a cause they consider an injustice or bad idea, they can't seem to let it go. Colleagues and superiors have noticed and have commented on this behavior, sometimes derisively. What is the problem here and what, if anything, do you do?

11. One of your employees has the habit of discussing their disagreements with you with your boss. You have known this for some time but have said nothing. Now you have made a decision affecting your entire organization and this individual has gone to your boss seeking a reversal. Your boss has done nothing, nor have they spoken to you about it. What, if anything, do you do now and why?

12. One of your employees seems determined to debate with you about any issue you raise during your staff meetings. Is this a problem and if so, what do you intend to do about it?

13. You believe your boss is about to make a decision likely to prove a big mistake. You are convinced the decision will have a negative impact on many people, especially those entrusted to your management skills. What do you do?

14. Your staff is aware you have reservations about the wisdom of a top management course of action that has now become a corporate decision. As a member of the corporate management team, senior management expects you to give the decision your full support and to help your staff make the necessary adjustments. It is time to announce the final decision to your staff and you are certain some of them would appreciate a bit of sarcasm and perhaps "slow-rolling" on your part. Your staff is listening.

15. Over the past six months, you made some difficult decisions, unpopular among many of your staff. You fully discussed these issues with all your employees – both individually and as a group – before making the decisions.

You carefully considered their input. Now the atmosphere in your organization has cooled and several of your employees seem determined to avoid unnecessary interaction with you. You are concerned this situation if it continues, might undermine teamwork and morale. What do you intend to do?

16. One of your low performing employees has applied for a new job. You receive a phone call from his prospective new boss asking for an honest and candid evaluation. Being honest could undermine his chances of moving on. What do you say and why?

17. Several of your newest employees tell you they do not believe you are giving them challenging enough assignments. They claim you always favor those with more seniority when it comes to opportunities, and this is hindering their career advancement. They tell you they believe your behavior encourages their more experienced colleagues to ignore their mentoring responsibilities. How do you respond and what will you do next? These new employees are standing in front of you.

18. You are a trusting manager. You endeavor to give your staff considerable latitude and freedom to accomplish their assignments in a manner best suited to their preferred working styles. You care about results not the how. You believe everybody understands their responsibility regarding the organization's time and attendance requirements. Today, two of your employees confront you with the allegation that one of your top performers is cheating the organization out of the required work hours. What is your approach to time and attendance requirements and what will you do with this allegation?

19. You are determined your organization must function as a high performing, interdependent team. You want every individual fully engaged, aware of what each other is doing and has to contribute, and confident their individual contributions are valued. How do you intend to make this happen? What steps will you take?

20. The word on the street involves the merger of two units with similar responsibilities. You hope they will select you to manage this merger. The former heads of the merged units might end up working for you. If you are offered the job, how will you manage this challenge? What specific steps will you take from the outset?

21. Two of your employees have come to you separately to complain about the other. Neither has asked you to intervene. You have observed this interpersonal clash is having a negative impact on their ability to effectively collaborate and on their team's working environment and product quality. You deem their collaboration essential to team success. What will you do?

22. You have an employee who is very bright and technically extremely skilled. Her individual work is excellent. However, when it comes to her interpersonal skills and sense of appropriate professional behavior, she often ruffles feathers and provokes disharmony. During a recent team briefing attended by senior management she said several things way out of line and inappropriate in your view. Do you believe you should do something about this? If so, what will you do and why?

23. Against the advice of several experienced individuals in your organization, you made and implemented a decision you were convinced was the correct thing to do. Two months have passed. During a staff meeting, those who opposed your action confront you with evidence that your decision is not having the desired effect. The evidence is compelling. How should you respond in front of your entire organization? You are sitting in their presence.

24. You took your current job filled with enthusiasm and some big ideas about how to take your organization in a new and more productive direction. You have had the opportunity to accurately assess the collective skills and talent you inherited. You conclude there is a mismatch between your goals and what your employees can accomplish now. How could you really screw up this situation? How will you manage to move forward?

25. You took your current job filled with enthusiasm and some big ideas about how to take your organization in a new and more productive direction. You have had the opportunity to accurately assess the collective skills and talent you inherited. You conclude you inherited the biggest group of free spirits in the organization. They are full of bright ideas about how to accomplish things and seem to share the notion that you should simply give them a general sense of what you want and get out of the way. They are bright and talented, but short on longevity and organizational experience. They believe the less you manage them the better. How could you really screw up this situation? How will you manage to move forward?

26. A member of your staff apparently ignored a direct order you gave him to undertake a specific action. You confront this individual, lose your temper, raise your voice in anger and say a few things you now regret. This incident is bothering you because it was out of character, excessive in emotional display, and you never asked for any explanation for his inaction. You just got mad. The employee seemed bewildered at your response. What if anything should you do?

27. Managers are entitled to hold and conduct meetings. Your employees are required to attend whether they enjoy them or not. You wish your meetings to be productive and for participants to feel they have value. What is your philosophy regarding effective meetings and how you should conduct them?

28. One of your worst professional nightmares has occurred. You're under pressure by your superiors to take an action you believe is wrong, perhaps unethical, even of questionable legality. Have you mentally prepared for this eventually? What do you intend to do?

29. You woke up this morning with the strong feeling it is time for you to move on; time for a new job or a new challenging experience. How should you pursue this instinct with your management? How do you take action without suggesting to your employees that you are tired of them or board with the work? What are you going to do?

30. You have been working hard for almost a year to address the performance shortfalls of an employee. Nothing has worked. The employee is clearly not meeting minimal standards for their pay grade and level of responsibility. You are growing frustrated, and frankly resent the amount of time required to deal with this employee's unchanging performance problems. What should you do now and why?

31. From your perspective, an employee sometimes seems overly friendly with you in your various interactions. While you have had an occasional working lunch with them in your building's cafeteria during which you discussed business matters, you are surprised when they suggest a dinner together this coming weekend. How do you respond and why?

32. During your vacation, the employee you left in charge and fully empowered to act in your absence made and implemented a decision with which you disagree. It is bothering you. What exactly did you delegate before leaving and how will you handle this situation?

10.

Measuring Your Growth

Without propere self-evaluation, failure is inevitable.

John Wooden, Legendary UCLA basketball coach

I will end this book with one last true story and a list of the ten mistakes you can count on making as a manager. There are valuable lessons to be gleaned in each.

First, the story. *A senior manager **asked** a subordinate manager to please reassign two of his employees to another unit in need of additional talent. The subordinate, protective of his turf, refused saying, "if you are only **asking** if I will do it, I will not. If you **order** me to do it, I will." The senior manager stubbornly refused to make it an order and the subordinate manager stubbornly refused to comply. Consequently, the reassignment never occurred, the relationship between the two managers soured, and the junior manager's organization suffered as a result of subtle retribution by his boss.*

I tell this story because it is a fabulous example of what the best managers never do. The best managers are flexible enough to avoid the stubbornness and foolishness that prevents them from doing their job.

The junior manager should have been flexible enough to interpret a legitimate request as a de facto order from a superior and, after some discussion, complied with the request. Compliance was his job. The senior manager should have done his job by simply saying *OK, I order you to reassign these two people*. Making certain the reassignment happened was the superior's job.

Now the ten mistakes. If you wish to take stock of how much growth and learning you are experiencing as a manager, here are the 10 mistakes you will without doubt make at some point in your managerial career. Like it or not these mistakes are inevitable because the job is extremely hard and you are human. I recommend you review this list once a year. It should provide you with a humbling laugh, whereas frequent repetitions of the same mistakes most certainly should not.

1. You will fail to delegate matters better left to your employees. Consequently, you will overwork and probably do an inferior job.

2. You will unnecessarily micromanage some things others could have done quite well without you. They are likely to be irritated.

3. You will fail to arrange your priorities correctly, leaving something important left undone. You will hear about it and feel stupid.

4. You will fail to keep your boss sufficiently informed about something that matters. They will be unhappy and will tell you so, affording you another reason to feel stupid.

5. You will fail to make a decision you should have made and there will be negative consequences. You will beat yourself up over this.

6. You will make at least one, if not more, failed attempts to please everyone. You will leave many people unhappy.

7. You will attempt to answer some questions, or violate a confidence, when silence or "I don't know," or "I'm not at liberty to say" would have been the better choice. It will be too late. Better hope you have done no great harm and made somebody really mad.

8. You will get beyond your managerial competence at least a few times and make some mistakes you will regret.

9. You will act on a false assumption with negative consequences. I hope that you fixed things fast.

10. You will pull your punches – that is, be less than candid – with more than one employee and superior. You will not like yourself afterwards and feel cowardly.

Irish explorer Robert McClure believed that *adventure equals risk plus purpose.* There is simply no way to get better at being a manager than through experience. Generally, our failures teach us the most powerful lessons.

Perhaps, at some point, you may conclude that a manager's job is not for you. In that case, it is certainly OK, if not profoundly wise from a professional, psychological, and physiological perspective, to opt out for some other professional endeavor. But you will not know until you have tried.

About the Author

Terry Joseph Busch, Ph.D has over forty years of broad professional experience as a teacher, international affairs analyst, manager, senior executive, consultant, and public speaker. His early work experience included stints as an Army Medical Services Corps Officer in Germany and Vietnam, and an Assistant Professorship in the Political Science Department at Denison University in Ohio. His distinguished career with the Central Intelligence Agency included senior assignments as Director of Leadership Analysis in the Directorate of Intelligence, Deputy Inspector General, and Director Human Resource Management. He is now President and CEO of his own management consulting practice.

CPSIA information can be obtained
at www.ICGtesting.com
Printed in the USA
LVOW10s1158260218
567888LV00002B/494/P